DÉLICES DE FRANCE

APPETIZERS

DÉLICES DE FRANCE

APPETIZERS

DINE WITH FRANCE'S MASTER CHEFS

KÖNEMANN

Acknowledgements

We would like to thank the following people and businesses for their valuable contributions to this project:

Baccarat, Paris; Champagne Veuve Clicquot Ponsardin, Reims; Cristallerie de Hartzviller, Hartzviller; Cristallerie Haute-Bretagne, Paris; Établissements Depincé Laiteries Mont-Saint-Michel, Saint-Brice; FCR Porcelaine Daniel Hechter, Paris; Harraca/Roehl Design, Paris; La Verrerie Durobor, Soigny (Belgium); Le Creuset Fonte Émaillée, Fresnoy-le-Grand; Renoleau, Angoulême; Maison Mossler Orfèvre Fabricant, Paris; Manridal, Wasselonne; Moulinex, Bagnolet; Pavillon Christofle, Paris; Porcelaine Lafarge-Limoges, Limoges; Porcelaines Bernardaud, Limoges; Porcelaines de Sologne et Créations Cacharel, Lamotte-Beuvron; Porcelaines Raynaud, Limoges; Rémy & Associés Distribution France, Levallois-Perret; Robert Havilland et C. Parlon, Paris; SCOF, St-Rémy-sur-Durolle; Tupperware, Rueil-Malmaison; Villeroy & Boch, Garges-lès-Gonesse; Zanussi CLV Système, Torcy.

Level of difficulty of the recipes:

★   easy

★★   advanced

★★★   challenging

© 1997 Original edition: Fabien Bellahsen, André Delmoral, Daniel Rouche
Original title: Délices de France, Entrées Chaudes, Abats, Légumes
Photographs: Michel Tessier
Wine recommendations: Georges Ciret
(Member of the Association of Professional Sommeliers)

© 1999 for the English edition
Könemann Verlagsgesellschaft mbH
Bonner Straße 126, D-50968 Cologne

Translation from French: Clèmence Scouten
English-language editor: Bessie Blum
Coordination and typesetting: Agents – Producers – Editors, Overath
Reproduction: Reproservice Werner Pees
Production manager: Detlev Schaper
Printing and binding: Leefung Asco Printers, Hong Kong

Printed in China

ISBN 3-8290-2743-5

10 9 8 7 6 5 4 3 2 1

Contents

Acknowledgements
4

Forewords
6

Recipes
8

Basic Recipes
222

Glossary
236

The Participating Chefs
238

Index of Recipes
239

Foreword

Dining culture is an art that draws people together and fosters harmony. A nation's cuisine is without doubt one of the most important values of any developed civilization, and familiarity with "foreign food" contributes—perhaps even more than we realize—to increased tolerance and mutual understanding between different cultures.

The sixteenth-century French poet Rabelais was well aware of this as he wrote in his novel *Pantagruel*, "Every rational human being who builds a house starts with the kitchen...." And before setting off for the Congress of Vienna in 1815, the French foreign minister Talleyrand reminded his king, Louis XVIII, "Sire, I need pots far more than instructions...."

Thus it is a special pleasure to introduce the *Délices de France* series, a collaborative effort involving many of the preeminent chefs working in France today. Almost 100 masters of their trade are gathered in these comprehensive collections of recipes, representing various geographical regions and branches of the culinary arts that have made French cuisine so renowned: bakers and pastry chefs, chocolatiers, sommeliers, and many more.

All the contributors have already made a name for themselves, or are well on their way to doing so. With its wealth of practical details and background information, *Délices de France* will appeal to anyone with culinary interests—from the hobby cook looking to impress guests at a dinner party to the experienced gourmet interested in improving their craft.

Roger Roucou
1988 President of the *Maîtres Cuisiniers de France*

Chefs' Foreword

For perhaps the first time in history, the *Délices de France* series has gathered the recipes of a large number of well-known chefs in a comprehensive collection of the delicacies of French cuisine. French cooking is revered throughout the world, and we believe that this portion of our cultural heritage, which so greatly enhances the joy and pleasures of life, is one of which we can be proud.

The cookbooks in this series offer a broad panorama of carefully selected culinary delights, and seek to build a bridge between experts from the various gastronomic professions and all friends of fine dining. It gives us, the chefs, the possibility to set down our expertise in writing and to disseminate our professional secrets, thus enriching and furthering the Art of Cooking. Once a luxury, *haute cuisine* is no longer limited to the patrons of elegant restaurants. The recipes presented here range in difficulty from straightforward to quite complex, and are intended to offer you ideas and encouragement in the preparation of your daily meals.

Allow yourself to be inspired! In this collection you will find novelties, acquaint yourself with regional and exotic specialties, and rediscover old favorites. There is a strong continuity between these recipes and the great tradition of French cooking—a rich and varied table offering a broad palette of gourmet pleasures ranging from the simple and light to the extravagant. We have dedicated our lives to this cuisine and are delighted to invite you on this voyage of culinary exploration.

We have made the details in the recipes as clear as possible in order to make it easier to try them at home. In this process, we illustrate our art, which provides a treat both for the palate and for the eye—two pleasures that go hand-in-hand in cooking. With a little practice, you will soon be skilled enough to turn the everyday into the extraordinary, and to impress your guests with culinary masterpieces.

In a special way, the Art of Cooking fosters the social, interpersonal side of life: It is no coincidence that food accompanies all the important milestones of our lives, from a family sitting down together at the table, to holiday celebrations and weddings, to business deals and political meetings.

We are pleased to present you with our most successful creations, so that you can share their pleasures with your loved ones. And we hope that you will have as much fun trying out these recipes as we did creating them.

Furthermore, we hope that the culinary specialties presented in *Délices de France* may serve as an ambassador throughout the world for the enjoyment and pleasures of life, and that this book may in some way contribute both to mutual understanding among cultures and to the refinement of culinary delights.

Good luck in trying out the recipes!
From the chefs of *Délices de France*

Belgian

1. In a large pot, bring salted water to a boil. Add the endives and the juice of one lemon. Add the sugar to cut the endives' bitterness. Cover and simmer.

Ingredients:
4 endives
1 lemon
1 tsp sugar
6½ tbsp/100 g butter
6½ tbsp/50 g flour
3 cups/750 ml milk
nutmeg
4 slices boiled ham
3½ oz/100 g Swiss
  cheese, grated
salt and pepper

Serves 4
Preparation time: 45 minutes
Cooking time: 15 minutes
Difficulty: ✷

2. Melt the butter in a large saucepan. Add the flour. Stir well to produce a roux. Do not let the mixture darken. In a separate saucepan, heat the milk until it just begins to boil.

Endive comes to us historically from Belgium, where it is also known as "witloof" (white leaf). It is also sometimes called "chicons" because it is related to chicory. You now know as much as our chef!

One suggestion: One should always add sugar to the water when boiling endive in order to reduce its natural bitterness. Once cooked, the endive will be saturated with water. It should be drained carefully and gently pressed to eliminate excess water. The endive should then be placed on some kind of absorbent material such as paper towel. Each endive is then wrapped in a thin slice of ham, producing perfect rolls. One last tip: The roll should be laid with the outer edge of the ham facing down so that it will stay closed. For the béchamel sauce, the hot milk should always be poured onto the cold roux or the cold milk onto the hot roux to prevent lumps.

This recipe is a classic that you may already know, though you may have forgotten it. It is almost a pleasure to burn one's tongue biting into this perfect winter dish. Simple and delicious, it is easily warmed up. It is a delightful accompaniment to any relaxed family meal, especially on a dark, stormy night with a bright fire blazing in the fireplace.

In order to enhance this winter meal, our wine expert recommends a Cahors to add structure and substance.

3. For the béchamel sauce, once the roux has cooled and the milk is hot, pour in a portion of the milk. Beat vigorously, especially at first, to eliminate any small lumps, then add the rest of the milk and bring to a boil. Add salt, pepper, and a pinch of nutmeg.

4. Roll the cooked and drained endives in the slices of ham. Place the rolls in a pre-buttered dish.

Endive

5. Gently cover the rolls with the béchamel sauce.

6. Grate the cheese over the endives and dot generously with butter. Bake at 350 °F for 15 minutes. Serve piping hot.

Maroilles

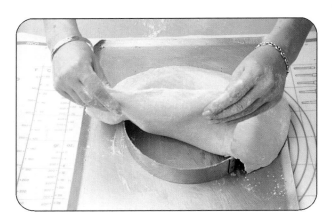

1. *Prepare the pastry according to the basic recipe. Roll it out and ease it into a flan ring or springform pan set on a greased baking sheet.*

Ingredients:
10½ oz/300 g short pastry (see basic recipe)
½ Maroilles
7 oz/200 g cream cheese
2 eggs
salt and pepper

Serves 4
Preparation time: 15 minutes
Cooking time: 30 minutes
Difficulty: ✳

2. *Remove the rind from the Maroilles, add the cream cheese, and mix the two together thoroughly.*

Maroilles is a soft-ripened, stripped, orange-crusted, cow's milk cheese, named for an abbey in Thiérache, France. Supple and creamy, it has a strong aroma and distinct taste. Today production of this cheese is controlled by the government, as is that of wine. The French term for this is *appellation d'origine controlée*. Where Maroilles is unavailable, one may substitute other rind-washed cheeses, such as a European Muenster. This recipe is also useful for using up any leftover cheese.

A very fresh cheese will combine more thoroughly with the cream cheese. If you have difficulty blending the two cheeses by hand, there is no harm in using an electric mixer. The cream cheese should not be whipped and one should choose a brand with as little water as possible.

The Maroilles pie is served warm, with buttered toast and a crisp green salad. It is delicious! The pie is very easily reheated and served as a leftover. Its distinct taste adds a delightful spice to dinner parties that is sure to be appreciated by one's guests.

Our wine expert advises that the aggressive flavor of Maroilles needs to be tamed. Her recommendation: Serve a good marc.

3. *Add the eggs. Beat until completely blended.*

4. *Pierce the pastry gently with a fork.*

Flan

5. Add a pinch of salt and pepper to the cheese and egg mixture.

6. Pour the cheese mixture into the pan. Bake at 350 °F for 30 minutes.

Single-Crust

1. Bring to a boil a large pot of salted water. After thoroughly cleaning the leeks, cut them in half where the green, leafy part begins. Poach both the stalk and the greens.

Ingredients:
2.2 lbs/1kg leeks
1 tbsp butter
10½ oz/300 g short pastry (see basic recipe)
4 eggs
6½ tbsp/100 ml heavy cream
6½ tbsp/100 ml milk
salt and pepper

Serves 4
Preparation time: 20 minutes
Cooking time: 40 minutes
Difficulty: ✲

2. Melt the butter in a sauté pan and lightly brown the leeks. Add salt and pepper. Allow to cool.

There is nothing quite so "French" as strolling through an outdoor market with leeks peeking out of your shopping basket. This vegetable is, plain and simply, a *sine qua non* of fine cuisine. Already popular in the times of the Egyptians and Hebrews, it was also widely enjoyed throughout the Roman Empire. Legend has it that the Emperor Nero himself ate great quantities of leeks to improve his voice; this earned him the moniker of a "porrophage," which we might loosely translate into modern idiom as "leekaholic."

Leeks are a diuretic; they are also a good source of fiber, mucilage, minerals, sulfur, and vitamin A. The leek is a wonderful vegetable—very light and with a gentle taste.

Our chef suggests that the leeks be well cooked so that they melt in the mouth. If they are too crisp, they may break the crust of the pie when the time comes to serve it.

It is important to keep an eye on the oven temperature during baking. This pie should cook slowly and the batter must never be allowed boil, otherwise the ingredients could separate. Just in case, one might add a teaspoon of cornstarch as a preventive measure. Other bulbous vegetables such as onions or fennel may be substituted for the leeks, or added to them, for variety.

The pie should be served warm and can easily be reheated, though it is unlikely that any would be left over when the dish is first served.

Our wine expert suggests that the aromatic undertones of a Savennières create an ideal accompaniment.

3. Prepare the short pastry according to the basic recipe. Roll it out and ease the dough into a tart pan or pie plate. Pierce gently with a fork. In a separate bowl, prepare the batter by mixing the eggs and the cream. Add salt and pepper.

4. Add the milk to the egg and cream mixture and whisk vigorously.

Leek Pie

5. Arrange the cooled leeks in the tart pan.

6. Pour the batter over the leeks. Bake at 350 °F for 30 minutes. Serve warm.

1. Very carefully separate the kidneys from their protective fat and, if necessary, remove the large nerve. Add salt and pepper. Peel and cut the potatoes as desired.

Ingredients:
2 veal kidneys
2.2 lbs/1 kg potatoes
⅓ cup/80 g butter
4 tbsp oil
6½ tbsp/100 ml
   juniper brandy (gin)
1 tbsp juniper berries
1 beef bouillon cube
¾ cup/200 ml warm
   water
salt and pepper

Serves 4
Preparation time: 30 minutes
Cooking time: 35 minutes
Difficulty: ✶

2. Blanch the potatoes in lightly salted water, then drain. Cook in a frying pan with ⅓ of the butter and half of the oil. Add salt and pepper to taste.

There are many different ways to prepare kidneys, some of which are detailed in this book. In this case, the kidney adopts a distinctive flavor based on the use of juniper in two forms: alcohol and berry. The slightly peppery and resinous taste of these black berries is often found in traditional cooking of Scandinavian countries, where it is greatly appreciated. Indeed, the originality of this recipe will not fail to astound you. While at first glance the combination of flavors seems unusual, it is always gratifying to stroll off the beaten path and explore a new taste.

It is essential that the kidneys be cooked properly. To prevent them from spitting back water, they must be firmly seared.

To blanche the potatoes, drop them in cold water and then bring to a boil. This will allow them to keep a firm consistency. They should be well-drained before browning in the frying pan. Also, the salt should not be added immediately or it would darken them. The kidneys should be cut at the last minute to allow them to conserve all their juice. Serve very hot and enjoy!

Kidneys with Juniper is a very delicate dish with a beautiful aroma. Its elegance is well suited to small dinner parties or perhaps an intimate dinner for two.

Our wine expert knows when to leave well enough alone. The flavor of juniper is so delicate that it easily overpowered by wine. He recommends beer instead, although one might try a good Côtes-du-Rhônes, such as a red Hermitage.

3. In another frying pan, heat the rest of the oil and one tablespoon of butter. Sear the kidneys, turning them so that they cook evenly. Kidneys should remain slightly pinkish.

4. Drain excess fat from the frying pan. Heat the remaining sauce in the pan, then add the juniper berries and the juniper brandy. Bring to a light boil.

Juniper

5. In a separate saucepan, melt the bouillon cube in the warm water. Bring to a boil and pour into the frying pan. Reduce mixture to ¾ its original volume.

6. Once reduced, add salt and pepper to taste. Whisk in the remainder of the butter vigorously. Serve the kidneys with this juniper sauce and the potatoes.

Clams à la

1. Peel and finely chop the shallots. Place them in a large pot and add the thyme and peppercorns.

Ingredients:
2 shallots
4 sprigs of thyme
whole peppercorns to
    taste
4½ lbs/2 kg little-neck
    clams
¾ cup/200 ml white
    wine
3½ tbsp/50 g butter
salt to taste

Serves 6
Preparation time: 5 minutes
Cooking time: 10 minutes
Difficulty: ✶

2. Thoroughly wash the clams and add them to the pot.

While Europeans may find the little-neck clams used in this recipe only in the Mediterranean, where they are called *clovisses* or *palourdes*, North Americans will find them in abundance on both the Atlantic and Pacific coasts. As with all shellfish, even with modern transportation and refrigeration, it is safer to eat clams only in "r" months—not during the hot summer months—unless you know they are fresh. The tell-tale sign of an aging clam is a loose seal; yawning clams do not deserve to be served at your table! Best of all are local clams in season, or freshly dug from sandy beaches. There is nothing quite like enjoying the winter's own bounty of *fruits de mer*!

It takes very little time to cook clams, barely five minutes. Keep an eye on the pot lid: As soon as it begins to rise a little with the steam from the boiling water, the clams are ready. If the clams continue cooking, they will become hard and chewy.

Mussels, another readily available mollusc, and cousin of the clam, may be sustituted for the little-necks or added to them. One may also add variety with salt water or bay scallops. To experiment with a spicier version of this dish, substitute basil, chopped tomatoes, and hot peppers for the thyme.

This is a perfect dish for any festive dinner menu and these clams are sure to please the heartiest seafood lover.

Our wine expert recommends a bottle of white Coteaux du Languedoc.

3. Add the white wine and a pinch of salt. Cover and cook on very high heat for about four or five minutes. Remove the clams from the pot as soon as they have opened; retain the liquid.

4. Arrange the clams in a serving dish. Pour the liquid through a sieve and bring to a boil.

Marinière with Thyme

5. Add the butter and beat well. Add salt or pepper if desired.

6. Pour the sauce onto the clams and serve very hot.

Vegetables

1. Peel and thinly slice the potatoes and onions.

Ingredients:
1½ lbs/700 g potatoes
2 medium onions
1 bouquet garni
1 lb/500 g tomatoes
2 red peppers
10 tbsp/150 g butter
3 cups/750 ml stock
  from a bouillon
  cube
olive oil
½ cup plus 2 tbsp/150
  g sour cream
1¾ oz/50 g Swiss
  cheese, grated

Serves 6
Preparation time: 20 minutes
Cooking time: 40 minutes
Difficulty: ✳

2. In a buttered ceramic baking dish, lay out all the potatoes and onions and sprinkle with the bouquet garni.

A visit to the Languedoc region of southwestern France is well worth the trouble of straying off the beaten path, especially for the wonderful vegetables produced in this area. In fact, it would be a crime to miss it.

In the south of France, gratins are prepared in an earthenware dish called a *tian*. In some regions, the words *tian* and *gratin* are interchangeable.

The preparation of this vegetable gratin involves nothing unusual. The chef's only caveat is to let the it cook for forty minutes, uninterrupted. Do not open the oven to check on it; the potatoes need all the heat and time they can get to become soft throughout. Do not let curiosity kill your gratin. When baked, the potato is a nutritious and satisfying food. This recipe can be varied by adding zucchini, eggplant, or broccoli. Almost any vegetable would be flattered to be presented in this manner. Remember to cut thin slices so they will cook well.

The bouquet garni is often available in a commercially prepared package; if not, it may be made from a combination of parsley, thyme, and bay leaves, with other aromatic herbs to suit the cook's taste, such as sage, rosemary, or savory.

Serve the gratin piping hot, just as it begins to brown. It is an excellent side dish with any grilled meat. The entire meal will be tasty and particularly wholesome.

This gratin comes from a land of warmth and sunshine and is complemented by a gentle wine. Treat it to a red Bandol (Domaine Ott).

3. Thinly slice the tomatoes and layer them on top of the potatoes and onions.

4. Roast the red peppers to make it easier to remove their skin. Peel, then cut lengthwise into strips.

au Gratin

5. Criss-cross the red peppers on top of the tomatoes. Dot the layer of peppers generously with the butter. Ladle on just enough stock to cover the vegetables, but no more. Add a little olive oil.

6. Add the sour cream and then sprinkle on the cheese. Bake for forty minutes at 300 °F. Serve hot.

Duck Foie Gras with

1. Peel the onion and press the clove into it. Place it in a pot of water along with the carrot and the bouquet garni. Let simmer.

Ingredients:
1 onion, 1 carrot
1 or 2 whole cloves
1 bouquet garni
3½ oz/100 g fresh salt
  pork
1 cup/100 g small
  (button) onions
sugar
13 tbsp/200 g butter
½ cup chopped shallots
¾ cup/200 ml ruby port
1 veal bouillon cube
truffle juice
1½ cups/250 g green
  Puy lentils
14 oz/400 g foie gras
1 bunch of chives
1 bunch of chervil
salt and pepper

Serves 4
Preparation time: 30 minutes
Cooking time: 45 minutes
Difficulty: ✲✲

The success of this recipe lies in the foie gras. The best foie gras is found in specialty shops, from November through May, and has a firm and smooth consistency.

For a long time, lentils were considered a common staple for common people. Particularly in combination with the potent and distinctive flavor of truffles lent by a bit of truffle juice in this recipe, however, the lentil proves itself utterly worthy of the foie gras, a traditionally aristocratic food. The green Puy lentil comes from the Velay region in south-central France.

As you may already know, when cooking any dried beans or legumes, salt should never be added until later; when added in the beginning, it will slow down the cooking process and may very well ruin the entire meal. Also, when the time comes to prepare the lentils, they should be placed in cold water which is then brought to a boil.

This dish should be served warm, as soon as you remove it from the stovetop. It should not be reheated or served as a leftover.

This warm dish will please any cultivated palate. The pleasant surprise any guest will experience with this meal demonstrates the perfection of the alliance of the lentils and foie gras. One of the most important rules from our wine expert is never to serve a wine with a high tannin content with foie gras. Obviously, the choice is yours, but we think you will enjoy a very fruity wine, such as a Volnay Champans.

2. Cut and blanche the salt pork. In a separate pot, caramelize the small onions small amounts of sugar, butter, and water. In a third pot, sauté the shallots in butter until they are nicely browned.

3. Add the port to the shallots and simmer gently. Dissolve the bouillon in a glass of water, pour into the shallots, and simmer until the sauce has reduced its volume by half. Stir in the rest of the butter and whisk energetically until the mixture is light.

4. Place the caramelized onions and the pork in the same pot and add a little truffle juice. Add the lentils. Gently stir while the mixture darkens. Salt if necessary. Set aside.

Green Puy Lentils

5. Cut the foie gras into slices and set them aside in a bowl filled with ice water. The slices will need to be patted dry before they are cooked.

6. In a nonstick pan, cook the slices of foie gras over high heat. Spread the lentils on a serving dish and lay out the foie gras slices attractively over the lentils. Pour the sauce over the whole dish and garnish with chives and chervil.

Zucchini

1. Prepare the pastry according to the basic recipe. Roll it out evenly and ease into a pie plate. Cut the ham into small pieces; cut the salt pork into long strips.

2. With a food processor, finely mince the salt pork and the veal.

3. Finely chop the onion and brown in the butter. Add the minced pork and veal. Peel the zucchini, but leave thin stripes of skin to create an alternating pattern of skin and pulp.

Ingredients:
10½ oz/300 g short pastry (see basic recipe)
3½ oz boiled ham
7 oz/200 g salt pork
7 oz/200 g boneless veal
1 onion
3½ tbsp/50g butter
2.2 lbs/1 kg zucchini
3 eggs
3 tbsp crème fraîche
3½ oz/100 g Swiss cheese, grated
1 tbsp chopped basil
1 tbsp chopped parsley
salt and pepper

Serves 8
Preparation time: 30 minutes
Cooking time: 40 minutes
Difficulty: ✶

During the Middle Ages and the Renaissance, gratins of this kind were known as *tourtes* and were highly esteemed. After the 17th century, they fell out of favor and were seldom made. The culinary arts in the ensuing centuries established their own standard of sophistication which they simply did not feel the gratin could meet, and chefs stopped serving it at their finest tables. Today, thank goodness, we are no longer so formal and can appreciate the charm of the countryside, in all its subtlety.

Originally, the word *tourte* meant "a rounded bread." In some regions large, round, heavy breads are still known by this name. In current culinary terms, a *tourte* consists of either short crust or puff pastry filled with any kind of meat, fish, or vegetable. In England, similar dishes are known simply as pies. Our chef recommends this recipe, which is as wonderful to consume as it is easy to prepare.

The only special requirement in preparing this gratin is a little tenderness, particularly when browning the onions and cooking the meats. If the onions become too dark, they will leave a bitter taste, and it is important to use a gentle hand in cooking the meats so that the different flavors will blend nicely. The *tourte* can be served hot or cold; either way, it is delicious. With a mesclun salad at its side, the Zuccini *Tourte* will provide a perfect meal. It can also be served as a light entrée on a warm summer night, or even packed into a picnic basket and carried along on a walk in the woods.

Our wine expert suggests a red Sancerre.

4. Add the zucchini and the ham to the onions, pork, and veal. Cover and cook for 10 minutes.

Tourte

5. Remove the meat and zucchini mixture from the heat. Beat the eggs with the crème fraîche and add. Stir in the grated cheese, the basil and parsley, and salt and pepper to taste.

6. Spread the cooled mixture in the pastry shell. Bake for 40 minutes at 350 °F.

Lamb Sweetbreads with

Ingredients:
1 lb/500 g string beans
1¼ lb/600 g lamb sweetbreads
1 beef bouillon cube
6½ tbsp/100 ml sherry
¾ cup/200 ml crème fraîche
6½ tbsp/100 g butter
salt and pepper

Serves 4
Preparation time: 25 minutes
Cooking time: 35 minutes
Difficulty: ✳

1. Remove the ends of the beans and poach them in slightly salted water. In a separate pot, bring salted water to a boil and blanche the sweetbreads.

2. In a nonstick pan, sauté the sweetbreads without oil or butter. Add salt and pepper. In a third pot, dissolve the bouillon cube in ¾ cup/200 ml water and bring to a boil.

Sweetbreads are the thymus glands of an animal, in this case the lamb, located near the top of the chest, in front of the windpipe. In adult animals, this gland atrophies. The longer, narrow part called the throat is inedible, but the round part, *la noix*, is delicious and prized by many gourmets.

Always rinse the sweetbreads under cold, running water to remove any undesirable impurities. Then wrap them carefully in a dish towel and press gently to give them a nice shape. If this is not done, they will become very dry and curl up as they cook. If you can find the French haricots verts, you will be delighted by their distinctive flavor, but the ordinary string bean will also make an excellent mousse. Cook the beans in an uncovered pot of boiling water. Salt the water at the last second, just before adding the beans. Salt speeds up the cooking process, which you can then halt by running the cooked beans under cold water. This prevents the beans from oxidizing and becoming discolored. Drain them immediately.

Sweetbreads are a delicate dish that will bring joy to the person serving them and to his or her lucky friends who get to eat them. They are also a wonderful part of an intimate dinner for two.

Our wine expert suggests a white St.-Joseph, which shares the rare and elegant features of the sweetbreads.

3. Deglaze the nonstick pan in which the sweetbreads were cooked with the sherry, and bring to a boil.

4. Pour the beef broth through a sieve and add to the sherry.

Green Bean Mousse

5. Pass the resulting sauce through a sieve. Add half the crème fraîche and let the mixture thicken over low heat. Add salt and pepper as needed. Add the butter and whisk vigorously.

6. In a food processor, blend the drained string beans and remaining crème fraîche until they become a homogenous mousse. Add salt and pepper as needed. Spread the mousse in the middle of a serving plate. Top with the warm sweetbreads and surround with the sauce.

Sea Kale with

1. Cut off the ends of the seak kale and gently wash the stalks.

Ingredients:
14 oz/400 g sea kale
½ chicken bouillon
 cube
6½ tbsp/95 ml water
juice of ½ lemon
3 egg yolks
10 tbsp/150 g butter
salt

Serves 4
Preparation time: 10 minutes
Cooking time: 20 minutes
Difficulty: ✴

2. Steam the sea kale until tender.

If you have never heard of sea kale, you are in for a treat. Also known as "Christmas asparagus," it is in a class by itself for its elegant shape and delicate taste.

Sea kale is a type of endive, a specialty of England and Scotland. The French have tried, mostly without success, to cultivate it in Brittany. Since 1982, it has been grown in laboratories where, like endive, it grows without light. It is still mainly found in specialty shops, but we remain hopeful that it will someday become more widely available.

Our chef has added a new twist to the classic hollandaise sauce by replacing water with chicken broth. The hollandaise sauce gains originality and flavor from this variation. Remember to melt the butter over very low heat and then stir while adding it to the hollandaise ingredients.

Boiling the lemon juice and the broth together reduces the acidity of the citrus. This also makes the taste of the sea kale much milder.

Do not forget to salt the water when steaming the sea kale. It should remain crisp. The best way to judge its readiness is to taste it.

As fast as it is attractive, as tasty as it is refined, this recipe is sure to become a favorite for dinner parties.

Sea kale, like asparagus, has a very delicate taste, subtle and precise. A smart choice of wine is a Xérès Fino.

3. Dissolve the bouillon cube in the water. Bring to a boil and add the lemon juice.

4. Place the egg yolks in a pot and pour in the chicken stock. Beat energetically. A thick, frothy sauce should develop. In a separate pot, melt the butter.

Hollandaise Sauce

5. Slowly pour the melted butter over the yolk and stock mixture, beating continuously. Add salt to taste. Set aside.

6. Place the sea kale on a serving dish. Serve warm with the hollandaise sauce.

Roasted Whole

1. Peel the tomatoes. Seed and dice two of them, and reserve until Step 5. Cut the remaining tomatoes into quarters.

Ingredients:
4½ lbs/2 kg tomatoes
2.2 lbs/1 kg large
  onions
1 bouquet garni
3½ tbsp/50 g butter
6½ tbsp/100 ml white
  wine
1 tbsp sugar
6½ tbsp/100 ml
  crème fraîche
4 veal kidneys
3 tbsp oil
parsley (optional)
salt and pepper

Serves 4
Preparation time: 40 minutes
Cooking time: 50 minutes
Difficulty: ✶✶

2. Peel and thinly slice 2 onions. Sauté, without browning them. Add 2 cups/500 ml water; season with salt and pepper. Stir in the tomato quarters. Add the bouquet garni and let simmer. Blend in a food processor, then strain.

The extraordinarily delicate taste of veal kidneys has become popular with gourmets around the world. The originality, personality, and perfect gastronomical balance of this recipe are bound to add to the general enthusiasm for veal kidneys.

The marriage of tomatoes and onions is always a great success. The tomato has many well-known virtues, but the lore of the onion is less a part of our culinary literacy. For instance, onions were the first and oldest vegetable to be deemed edible. They have also long been of medicinal interest because of their diuretic properties.

Flambé the wine as soon as it begins to boil in order to cook off the alcohol and minimize any acidity. The sugar added here also furthers this process.

After the onions have been puréed, warm them up with 2 tablespoons of crème fraîche; this will greatly improve their taste. Also, when the kidneys are done, pierce holes in them with the tip of a knife.

This is a tricky recipe, but not a difficult one. Remember that the kidneys cannot be rewarmed or eaten cold, though it is unlikely any will be left uneaten long enough to cool off at all.

Our wine expert suggests a wine from Burgundy with an aroma of red morello cherries, such as a Gevrey-Chambertin.

3. Thinly slice the remaining onions, then blanch. Drain them and allow to cool. In a large pot, melt 1/3 of the butter. Add the onions and half of the wine. Sprinkle with the sugar and let simmer. Flambé the wine when the first bubbles appear.

4. Once the onions have begun to soften, add the remainder of the wine. Salt lightly, add pepper, cover, and let simmer.

Veal Kidneys

5. When the onions are quite soft, purée in a food processor. Add the crème fraîche and return to low heat, stirring until well-blended. Set aside. In a separate pan, heat the tomato sauce from Step 2, stirring until thickened. Add the diced tomatoes.

6. Heat the oil and remaining butter in a large pan and roast the kidneys with salt and pepper. They should remain slightly pink. Spoon the onion mousse onto a serving dish and surround with the tomato sauce. Slice the kidneys and arrange on the sauce. Add fresh ground pepper if desired, and garnish with parsley.

Stuffed Cabbage

1. Clean the cabbage, the Swiss chard, and the sorrel thoroughly. Set aside 7 or 8 whole cabbage leaves, and finely chop the rest of the vegetables.

Ingredients:
2 heads of curly-leaf
   green cabbage
2 bunches of Swiss
   chard
14 oz/400 g sorrel
1 lb/500 g bacon
4 cloves of garlic
1 bunch of parsley
8 eggs
1 lb/500 g stale bread
2 cups/500 ml milk
2 chicken bouillon
   cubes
salt and pepper
1 net

Serves 6
Preparation time: 40 minutes
Cooking time: 2 hours
Difficulty: ✳

2. Blanch the whole cabbage leaves in a large pot of salted water. Be sure not to overcook them; they should remain slightly crisp. Combine the chopped sorrel, cabbage and chard in a large mixing bowl.

This ancient, earthy recipe has been revived here unchanged. Please note that the ingredients are those used by farmers a hundred years ago: garden vegetables, bacon, milk, and eggs. The call of the land heard from this dish is irresistible.

The stuffing saves up to ten days in the refrigerator and can be served cold or reheated; simply slice and sauté it. Because of its shelf life, this recipe is easily doubled and stored in anticipation of guests or for days when there is simply not enough time to cook.

After soaking in milk, the bread should be drained and pressed evenly to keep the stuffing from becoming too liquid.

It is important to slice the vegetables by hand; they will taste better. Machines tend to mash vegetables, which produces some acidity. The stuffing should be mixed by hand as well, to give the vegetables time to blend with each other as thoroughly as possible.

Grandmothers from the Charentais region of France would traditionally knit nets to tie up the stuffed cabbage. But not to worry, a net shopping bag will do perfectly well. This is a dish to be enjoyed by the family together; it suits all different tastes. Whether served cold or reheated, no one will pass up the chance to share this stuffed cabbage.

To do justice to this great stuffing, choose a wine from the Charentais region, such as a Saint-Sornin.

3. Chop the bacon, mince the garlic and parsley, and add all three to the mixing bowl with the greens.

4. Blend the eggs into the mixed greens and add salt and pepper. In a separate bowl, soak the bread in the milk. Drain the bread well to remove excess milk, then grind in a food mill over the mixing bowl. Combine all ingredients by hand.

à la Charentais

5. Place a net in a large strainer. Arrange the whole cabbage leaves to cover the net, then fill with the stuffing. Fold the cabbage leaves to cover the stuffing. Tie the net tightly to create a cabbage-like shape.

6. Dissolve the bouillon cubes in a large pot of boiling water. Add salt and pepper. Poach the stuffed cabbage for two hours over very low heat. Strain the cabbage and serve.

Calf's Liver

1. Finely chop the onions, and sauté them with the butter until they begin to sweat. Add the cognac and a little water. Let simmer.

Ingredients:
6 onions
3 tbsp/45 g butter
2 cups/500 ml
    cognac
1 cube beef bouillon
1 tsp/5 g sugar
4 slices calf's liver
⅓ cup/80 ml oil
1¾ oz/50 g lardon
juice of ½ lemon
3 baby carrots
salt and pepper

Serves 4
Preparation time: 15 minutes
Cooking time: 30 minutes
Difficulty: ✫

2. Dissolve the bouillon cube in the rest of the water, then add it and the sugar to the onions. Simmer for about 30 minutes, stirring occasionally.

In Charente, calf's liver is always served with onions, lard, cognac, or lemon. This tradition inspired our chef to bring together all these elements in a wonderful symbiotic dish that will fill any gourmet with happiness. Moreover, calf's liver is a richly nutritious food, full of iron, phosphorus, and vitamins A & B.

The key to successfully preparing the onion fondue is to allow it to cook over very low heat and to be sure that it always remains transparent. It can be stored up to eight days in the refrigerator, and thus can be prepared some time in advance. The liver can be cooked anywhere from rare to well done, according to individual preference.

Baby carrots are a wonderful accompaniment. They are very easy to prepare and add a perfect finishing touch to the dish.

The great variability of this dish will keep family dinners from ever becoming repetitive and will add an old country charm to your dinner parties.

The acidity of a Moulin-à-Vent, one of the best Beaujolais, is a welcome contrast to the delicate taste of the liver and onions.

3. Remove the thin outer layer of skin from the liver.

4. Heat the oil in a frying pan and sear the liver slices. Add salt and pepper as desired. Set the liver aside.

with Onion Fondue

5. In the same frying pan, brown the lardons and deglaze the pan with the lemon juice.

6. Add the onions to the lardons. Mix well. Place the liver slices on a serving platter and arrange the onion mixture in an attractive manner. Add the baby carrots as a finishing touch.

Char Mousse with

1. Remove the skin and bones from the fish steaks. Place the flesh and the eggs in a food processor and whip.

Ingredients:
2 lbs/900 g char or
   brook trout flesh
4 eggs
2 cups/500 ml crème
   fraîche
2 carrots
1 celery stalk
1 leek
13 tbsp/200 g butter
1 cup/250 ml port
salt and pepper

Serves 8
Preparation time: 25 minutes
Cooking time: 35 minutes
Difficulty: ✲✲

2. Add ¾ of the crème fraîche; salt and pepper as desired. Beat a few more seconds until the mousse has a smooth, homogeneous consistency.

Brook trout and char are two of the choicest fish in the salmonid family; either one will make a food lover's mouth water. How does one choose between the two? Our chef did not hesitate: His favorite is the *omble chevalier*, or char, one of the world's finest freshwater fish, found only in very deep lakes. No matter what variety you choose, the flavor of port wine enhances the sophisticated flavors of this method of preparation.

Each ingredient must be carefully measured, especially for the mousse; other than that, this recipe presents no particular difficulties. It will, however, demand your full attention.

The key to the mousse is its consistency: it should be a little springy, and not at all watery. It is important not to overbeat the mousse mixture. The accompanying sauce can be made just before being served. This delicious appetizer can be eaten hot or cold, and can be kept in the refrigerator for up to two days.

Oyster mushrooms make a nice accompaniment and are fairly readily available these days. Even simple cultivated mushrooms will go well here. This dish makes a colorful display: The mousse can be formed in creative size or shape molds to add distinction to any buffet table.

The bouquet of linden in Sauvignon grapes is a beautiful complement to the aroma of the salmon. Our wine expert's advises a bottle of Pouilly-Fumé to blend these flavors.

3. Generously butter a mold and pour in the mousse. Bake at 350 °F for 20 minutes.

4. Clean and peel the vegetables and cut them into long, thin slices à la julienne. In a sauté pan, sweat the julienne in a tablespoon or two of butter. Add a little water, and salt and pepper to taste. Do not overcook; the vegetables should remain crisp.

Vegetable Julienne

5. Over low heat, reduce the port to half its initial volume. Add the rest of the crème fraîche along with some salt and pepper. Allow the mixture to thicken.

6. Beat in the remaining butter. Season to taste. Unmold the mousse on a serving plate, pour the sauce around it and garnish as desired. Serve warm with the julienned vegetables.

Tongue and

1. Blanch the tongues and the sweetbreads for a few minutes in a pot of salted water. Drain and let cool.

Ingredients:
4 lamb's tongues
14 oz/400 g veal
   sweetbreads
8 carrots
8 pearl onions
1 bouquet garni
¾ cup/200 ml white wine
8 fresh new turnips
7 oz/200 g chanterelle
   mushrooms
1¾ oz/50 g green beans
¾ cup/100 g peas
1 bunch of chives
¾ cup/200 ml crème
   fraîche
10 tbsp/150 g butter
salt and pepper

Serves 4
Preparation time: 15 minutes
Cooking time: 40 minutes
Difficulty: ✶

The *navarin*, originally a lamb stew with potatoes, turnips and other vegetables, is a traditional and well-respected French dish, though few are aware of its history. Some say that it was created in honor of a naval victory by the French Navy and its allies during Greece's war of independence in a battle at Navarin, near Pylos. Others hold that this meal is much older, and that its name is actually a declension of the French word for turnip, *navet*, which was at the time one of the primary ingredients.

To keep them as white as possible, the sweetbreads should be rinsed under cold running water for a good amount of time.

The morsels of sweetbreads will lend thickness and flavor to the sauce. This original idea will be a pleasant surprise for any dinner guest. If you like the taste of the sweetbreads but do not care for their texture, they can be puréed in a food processor and added to the sauce, using a sieve to filter any small pieces of skin. This wonderful springtime dish, with its accompanying vegetables, will delight your guests. Our wine expert suggests a white Sauvignon. Bon appétit!

2. Peel and dice half the carrots and onions into a mirepoix.

3. Boil a pot of water. Add the mirepoix, bouquet garni, salt, and pepper. Stir in the wine. Cook the tongues in this preparation for about 30 minutes, then add the sweetbreads and continue cooking for another 20 minutes.

4. Peel and cut up the turnips, mushrooms green beans and the remaining carrots and onions. Poach the carrots and turnips in separate pots; boil the remaining vegetables together.

Sweetbread Navarin

5. Pour the tongue and sweetbread broth through a sieve. Reduce the broth to half its volume. Peel and dice the tongues; also dice the sweetbreads.

6. For the sauce, combine the diced sweetbreads with the crème fraîche in a large pot over medium heat and whip. Adjust seasoning. Add the butter and continue beating. Serve very hot with the vegetables.

Stuffed Cabbage

1. Cook the ground pork. Grind the bacon and ham. Thoroughly combine all 3 meats. Chop the onions, garlic and parsley and mix into the meats. Lightly salt and pepper.

Ingredients:
½ lb /250 g ground pork
1 lb/500 g bacon
3½ oz/100 g or 3 slices raw or cured ham
2 onions
2 cloves of garlic
1 bunch of parsley
1 cabbage
⅓ lb fatback
1 cube chicken bouillon
salt and pepper

Serves 6
Preparation time: 40 minutes
Cooking time: 40 minutes
Difficulty: ✷✷

2. Blanch the cabbage leaves in a large pot of salted water. Do not overcook; the leaves should remain crisp. Line a bowl with a dishtowel and then line the towel with sliced fatback, leaving enough hanging over the edge of the bowl to fold over the stuffing.

In the southwestern region of France, the cutting of a stuffed cabbage was a man's prerogative and a sign of his authority, so much so that it became an insult in the local vernacular to say that a man "is not cutting the stuffed cabbage!" Today, of course, anyone may cut the stuffed cabbage, keeping in mind that to do so is still an honor.

This delicious stuffed cabbage is named after the wonderful restaurant where it was created: *Belle Meunière*.

Our chef recommends removing and discarding the edges of the cabbage leaves, since they tend to be tough and difficult to digest.

The stuffing should be tasted and the seasoning adjusted before filling the cabbage. Usually all that is needed is a little pepper, since the fatback is already salted.

It is very important to respect the cooking time of the cabbage, which should be done over a low heat. If the stuffing is cooked too quickly, the meat tends to dry out while the inside remains uncooked. Served hot in the winter, chilled in the summer, as an appetizer or an entrée, this Stuffed Cabbage *à la Belle Meunière* adds a rustic touch in all seasons, on all occasions.

Our wine expert suggests a Cahors.

3. Place a layer of cabbage leaves on top of the fatback, also leaving enough to fold over the top. Fill with the meat stuffing, alternating with additional layers of cabbage leaves.

4. Fold first the cabbage leaves and then the fatback over the stuffing. Close the dish towel over the stuffed cabbage. The cabbage must be wrapped very tightly in the towel to keep its shape.

à la Belle Meunière

5. Dissolve the bouillon cube in 2 cups/500 ml water. Pour over the cabbage. Cover and let simmer over low heat for approximately 40 minutes.

6. Remove the towel and slice the cabbage. Serve warm, accompanied by a tomato coulis.

Chicken

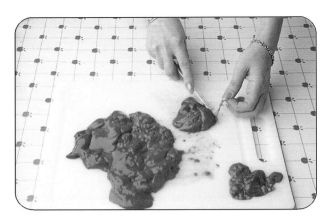

1. If necessary, carefully remove the nerves and skin from the livers, then cut into small pieces.

Ingredients:
7 oz/200 g chicken
   livers
5 tbsp/40 g flour
1 bunch of parsley
2 cloves of garlic
3 eggs
3 egg yolks
1⅔ cup/400 ml milk
¾ cup/175 ml crème
   fraîche
tomato coulis of your
   choice
black olives to
   garnish
salt and pepper

Serves 4
Preparation time: 15 minutes
Cooking time: 30 minutes
Difficulty: ✶

2. Put the liver in a blender or food processor. Add the flour and some salt and pepper. Blend for some time, until the mixture is completely smooth.

This charming old recipe, reminiscent of our grandmothers' cooking, has been adopted and revamped by our chef to appeal to a wider audience.

The first thing to do is to choose very nice livers. Turkey or any poultry livers may be substituted for the chicken livers. The nerves and any skin should be removed as completely as possible; they are often bitter, especially skin that has touched the gall bladder, and can ruin the whole meal.

It is important to blend the livers, flour, garlic and parsley very thoroughly so that the final paste is homogeneous and flavorful. The other ingredients should be added only once this mixture is completely blended. The oven should be set at 300 °F, and the liver cakes should never be allowed to boil.

Our chef has opted here for a tomato and olive coulis to go with the cakes, though a Madeira sauce or a Nantua sauce are also possibilities. The choice is yours.

This is an attractive and delicious dish, with the comforting taste we may remember from our grandmothers' tables. It is sure to liven up any meal.

Our wine expert suggests a Les Clos Chablis. This is one of the seven great Chablis, and it has been chosen for its remarkable smoothness.

3. Add the parsley and the garlic. Beat again. Do not be afraid to overbeat.

4. Add the whole eggs and egg yolks. Whip again.

Liver Cakes

5. Pour in the milk and crème fraîche. Beat at a slightly lower speed.

6. Pour the batter into pre-buttered molds. Cook them in a bain-marie in the oven at 350 °F for approximately 30 minutes. Unmold and serve hot with a tomato coulis. Garnish with olives.

Sautéed Tripe

1. Blanch the tripe in two changes of water. Slice the carrots and half the onions; halve the garlic. Place the vegetables, garlic, cloves, bouquet garni and tripe in a pot of salted water and simmer for 2½ hours.

Ingredients:
1 lb/500 g of plain
   tripe
10½ oz/300 g carrots
14 oz/400 g onions
1 bouquet garni
1 bulb of garlic
3 whole cloves
2 tbsp/30 g butter
6½ tbsp/100 ml
   vinegar
1¼ cup/300 ml white
   wine
parsley to garnish
salt and pepper

Serves 5
Preparation time: 40 minutes
Cooking time: 2 hours 30 minutes
Difficulty: ✶✶

2. Peel and thinly slice the rest of the onions. Once the tripe has cooled, slice it.

Tripe, or *gras double*, has not yet gained entry into the world of international haute cuisine. This recipe is a provincial one, but also one to be appreciated by refined palates. If, like our chef, you are fond of rustic simplicity, you will be delighted to discover a new way to prepare tripe. Once you have tried it, you will readily understand why it is so famous throughout the Lyon region.

Our chef recommends letting the tripe soak in slightly vinegary water for at least twelve hours. This should remove the tripe's sometimes unpleasant odor.

In general, this is not a recipe for anyone in a hurry. For those who have either less patience or less time, the normal 2½-hour cooking time can be shortened to about one hour by using a pressure cooker. In either case, pat the tripe dry after its initial cooking to remove excess water before sautéing.

This traditional Lyonnais meal is a regional favorite. It is even rumored to be the personal favorite of a certain government official (in the Lyons area), and who knows who else? Warm and sympathetic, this is a dish fit for a president. The tripe should be served immediately after cooking.

Our wine expert recommends a Pouilly-Fuissé or a Château-Chalon. This great, daring white wine has a particular energy that contrasts delicately with the softness of the tripe.

3. Divide the butter between 2 pans and add some oil to each. Brown the onions in one pan, the tripe in the other.

4. Add the browned onions to the tripe. Stir. Add salt and pepper.

à la Lyonnaise

5. Using the vinegar, deglaze the pan with the tripe and onions. Let the vinegar evaporate.

6. Pour in the white wine. Let all fluids evaporate until the pan is dry. Garnish the tripe with chopped parsley and serve.

Langoustine and

1. Separate the langoustine heads from the tails, then peel the tails. Carve the artichoke hearts and rub with a cut lemon.

Ingredients:
24 langoustines
4 artichoke hearts
2 lemons
1¼ cup/150 g flour
1 carrot
7 oz/200 g mushrooms
3½ oz/100 g celery root
1 black truffle
2 tsp/l0 ml olive oil
4 tsp/20 g butter
1 bunch of parsley
1 bunch of dill
salt and pepper
For the vinaigrette:
¼ cup/60 ml walnut oil
4 tsp/20 ml sherry
   vinegar
4 tsp/20 ml lemon juice
salt and pepper

Serves 4
Preparation time: 30 minutes
Cooking time: 25 minutes
Difficulty: ✶✶

A medley is nothing more than honest and sparkling cuisine. The delicate crustaceans allied with artichoke hearts in this recipe create a sense of refined originality, worthy of the best tables.

Our chef advises us that it is much easier to remove the inedible, hairy choke after cooking the artichoke hearts. Monitor the artichoke hearts as they are cooking by poking them with a very sharp knife. You can make them crisp or allow them to soften to melt in your mouth, according to taste. Once they are sliced, the artichoke hearts should be sautéed very rapidly and not allowed to brown, which would give them a bitter taste.

The langoustines, on the other hand, must be browned and crisp. Crayfish would also look lovely in this setting; they could be substituted for the langoustines just for fun.

The final touch, a stately black truffle finely sliced à la julienne, will lend its prestige and taste to this unforgettable meal, which is especially delightful during the winter holiday season. It is served warm.

The finesse and gentle taste of the soft langoustine meat will be stimulated by the rustic lightness of the slightly bitter artichokes. To round out the sensational experience, our wine expert suggests the flowery bouquet of a Savennières Clos-des-Papillons.

2. Bring a pot of slightly salted water to a boil. Blend the flour and a little water into a very smooth paste, then add to the boiling water with the juice of one lemon. Whisk well to avoid lumping.

3. Once this mixture is boiling, add the artichoke hearts and cook to the desired softness. Drain and allow to cool.

4. Cut the carrot, mushrooms, celery root, and truffle à la julienne. Slice the artichoke hearts very thinly.

Artichoke Medley

5. In a pan with the olive oil, sear the langoustine tails. Add salt and pepper. In a separate pan, sauté the artichoke slices. Top with the butter and set aside.

6. Combine the ingredients for the vinaigrette. Lay the artichoke slices in a circle on a serving dish and surround them with the langoustine tails. Fill the center with the julienned vegetables, and garnish with parsley and dill. Serve with the vinaigrette.

Light Spring

1. Clean and trim the green beans. Boil them in salted water, but do not overcook. Repeat with the turnips and zucchini. Drain the vegetables, douse in cold water, and set them aside.

Ingredients:
5¼ oz/150 g string beans
16 baby turnips (with stem)
1 zucchini
16 baby carrots (with stem)
1 cup/150 g peas
7 oz/200 g chanterelles
16 pearl onions
6½ tbsp/100 g butter
7 oz/200 g oyster mushrooms
2 sprigs of flat parsley
salt and pepper

Serves 4
Preparation time: 15 minutes
Cooking time: 20 minutes
Difficulty: ✳

2. Poach the carrots and the peas, and lightly blanch the chanterelles. Douse in cold water, then drain.

Healthy eating has assumed great importance in today's world, but it is still important for food to taste good! This recipe showcases vegetables served on their own. They offer a delightful range of color and a full complement of vitamins. Baby vegetables, more delicate and subtler than their full-grown kin, are preferred in this kind of recipe. There are many different kinds to choose from, and you might consider adding beans or asparagus to complete this rainbow of flavors.

The cooking time is very short and the vegetables will taste better if they retain most of their initial "crunch." Salting the cooking water enhances taste and also helps maintain the vegetables' color. They should be doused in cold water after removing them from the heat to halt the cooking process.

Devotees of lighter cooking can steam the vegetables and serve them without further ado, but if steamed vegetables are not to your taste, sauté them in butter. Our chef advises not to let them brown, lest they become bitter. One can prevent this by adding a spoonful of water when sautéing, but the vegetables should be drenched in butter, not water.

Vegetables are truly the salt of the earth and this recipe will show you why. The Light Spring Ragoût can stand on its own, but may also be served as an accompaniment to meat, fish, or poultry.

According to our wine expert, the balance of a Muscat d'Alsace will maintain harmony among all these different flavors.

3. Poach the onions in a pot of slightly salted boiling water. Cool them rapidly, drain, and set aside.

4. Just before serving the meal, drop the chanterelles into a frying pan with a little melted butter, and salt and pepper to taste.

Ragoût

5. Repeat in a separate frying pan with the oyster mushrooms.

6. Immediately before serving, melt the rest of the butter. Toss in the vegetables and stir gently. Sprinkle with salt and pepper. Arrange attractively on a serving platter and garnish with a few leaves of parsley.

Escargot Casserole

1. In a large bowl, sprinkle the sea salt on the snails and stir to distribute the salt evenly. Let the snails rid themselves of any impurities, then rinse generously with a solution of vinegar and water. Repeat 3 or 4 times.

2. Prepare a simple court-bouillon with the ingredients listed (see basic recipe). Season with salt and pepper. Let cool, then add the snails and bring to a boil.

Ingredients:
1 handful sea salt
2.2 lbs/1 kg snails
vinegar to rinse snails
1 onion
1 tbsp/15 ml oil
1½ cups /200 g sausage
    meat
1 tbsp tomato purée
1 tsp flour
¾ cup/200 ml white wine
4 cloves of garlic
2 tbsp chopped parsley
salt and pepper
For the court-bouillon:
(see basic recipe)
1 sprig of thyme
1 bay leaf
1 pearl onion
2 whole cloves

Serves 4
Preparation time: 40 minutes
Cooking time: 1 hour 30 minutes
Difficulty: ✶

Known variously as *cagouilles* in the southwest of France, *cacalaus* in Provence, and escargots throughout the world, snails are a hallmark of French cuisine. Supposedly, the English were at one time appalled by the consumption of escargots, though when they set foot on continental soil they appear to enjoy snails with as much gusto as anyone.

The escargot season is from April to September, when they are least expensive. Our chef recommends the native French petit-gris variety of snail, more easily found in the southwest of France, but also cultivated with increasing success in the United States.

Snails should always be placed in cold water and then brought to a boil; they should never be put in boiling water. It is necessary to repeatedly skim off the froth that forms during the boiling process.

To check whether the snails are done, remove one from the water and gently push the point of a knife into it. If you feel any resistance from the snail, it is not yet done. The snail is ready when it is easily removed from its shell.

For the sauce, any dry white wine will do. If the sauce becomes too thick, it may be diluted with a little water or bouillon.

The snails can be eaten warm or cold with vinaigrette. This original dish, prepared with love, smothered in a covered casserole, will reflect glory on any chef.

Our wine expert feels that the rich texture of the snail is a good partner for a sharp white wine like an Entre-Deux-Mers.

3. While the snails are cooking, peel the onion and mince very finely until it resembles a purée. Sauté in the oil until golden brown.

4. Stir the sausage meat into the onion purée and cook for 5 or 6 minutes. Then add the tomato purée.

à l'Entre-Deux-Mers

5. Add the flour and the white wine. Stir this mixture vigorously until well blended. Season with salt and pepper. Cook on low heat for a few minutes.

6. After the snails have simmered 45 minutes, strain them. Retrieve the thyme, onion, and bay leaf and add to the sausage, along with the garlic and chopped parsley. Simmer for 15 to 20 minutes. Serve hot.

Porcini and

1. Thinly slice the mushrooms and brown them in half of the butter. Salt and pepper to taste and set aside.

Ingredients:
3½ oz/100 g sliced
    porcini
½ cup/125 g butter
2.2 lbs/1 kg potatoes
1¾ oz/50 g grated
    Swiss cheese
salt and pepper

Serves 6
Preparation time: 15 minutes
Cooking time: 10 minutes
Difficulty: ✷✷

2. Peel the potatoes. Grate them into thin, toothpick-like pieces. Add salt and pepper.

Serving this wonderful combination of potatoes and mushrooms is a pure pleasure at any point in the course of a well-balanced meal. On its own, it may be the main dish in a wholesome dinner. It is also a great side dish for a dinner party, since it goes perfectly with any meat or wild game. For any palate, whether naive or discriminating, this pancake will satisfy any appetite.

Our chef suggests using old potatoes, since they lose less water during cooking. Even so, they must be pressed very firmly in a dishtowel after grating to remove as much water as possible. When you see and taste the final result, you will be glad you took the trouble. Potatoes are healthy, nutritious, and easy to digest. They are energizing and malleable, and in small quantities are a good food for diabetics and for those who must be careful about their caloric intake.

The marriage of porcini mushrooms and potatoes is a happy one, although many other varieties of mushroom could be used. Potatoes are flexible and go well with myriad partners. They will absorb the flavor of whatever mushroom you chose, wild or cultivated, and the effect will be delicious.

This pancake goes nicely in a picnic basket for an afternoon stroll. Kids love it and pickiness will be forgotten when you offer it up. Quick and inexpensive to prepare, it will come in handy when you are short on time.

Our wine expert suggests a sparkling wine such as the Rousette de Savoie.

3. Melt the rest of the butter in a large ovenproof frying pan. Press the grated potatoes in a dishtowel to remove as much water as possible, then carefully line the pan with about half the potatoes.

4. Sprinkle the grated cheese over the potatoes.

Potato Pancake

5. Distribute the mushrooms on top of the cheese.

6. Cover the mushrooms with a second layer of potatoes. Pack firmly. Bake at 350 °F, checking occasionally to make sure the pancake is not sticking to the pan. Flip it once or twice. Serve warm as a main or side dish.

Ingredients:
3½ oz/100 g morels
1 lb/500 g puff pastry
   (see basic recipe)
1 egg yolk
⅓ cup/80 g butter
⅔ cup/80 g flour
3 cups/750 ml milk
¼ tsp ground nutmeg
6½ tbsp/100 ml heavy
   cream
salt and pepper

1. Soak the morels in water. Roll out the puff pastry and cut a 6 in/15 cm square. With the excess pastry, roll out 2⅜ in/1 cm-wide strips to place around the edge of the square. Tie the ends together in a knot.

Serves 4
Preparation time: 25 minutes
Cooking time: 35 minutes
Difficulty: ✶

2. Dilute the egg yolk with a little water and brush it over the pastry.

This exquisite *feuilleté*, or puff pastry, light and golden brown, is always a hit. This recipe is a good opportunity to display your talents; it will charm any guest and reward the cook with a genuine triumph. It is not so very difficult, especially once the preparation is broken down into two parts. Our chef offers a few tips: Puff pastry will rise higher and be lighter if laid on a baking sheet that has been cooled in a freezer beforehand. The pastry can be prepared the night before and stored in the refrigerator. The end result will look as if it just arrived from the baker's, yet it came from your kitchen! Another impressive touch is to play with the shape of the pastry—cut out flowers or birds or hearts, or whatever your imagination decrees.

Once it is filled, puff pastry absorbs any liquid and will become soggy. The sauce, a simple béchamel sauce made with cream and finely chopped morels, should be poured into the pastry just before serving. Though our chef selected morels, one could also use another variety of mushroom, or even fish or ham, instead.

The art of entertaining lies in the elegance and freedom of the host or hostess. With a dish like this, you will not be tied to the kitchen and your guests will hardly realize the care the *feuilleté* demanded. Won't it be delightful to make such a grand impression?

It takes a great wine to embellish this marvelous pastry. Our wine expert suggests a Pomerol Château Mazeyres.

3. Bake the puff pastry at 350 °F for about 20 minutes. Clean the morels, then chop thoroughly in a food processor or blender.

4. Melt the butter in a frying pan. Mix in the flour to make a roux, stirring constantly. Do not let the roux brown. Once it is done, let cool. Heat the milk and pour onto the cooled roux, whisking well to prevent lumps. Salt and pepper lightly. Add the morels and cook over low heat.

Feuilleté

5. Remove the puff pastry from the oven. Cut off the top with a paring knife and hollow out the center.

6. Season the morel sauce with the nutmeg. Add the cream and stir until well blended. Bring just to a boil one last time. Fill the feuilleté with the sauce, replace the top crust, and serve.

Thrush

Ingredients:
5¼ oz/150 g foie gras
1 lb/500 g sausage
  meat
3½ oz/100 g
  prosciutto
12 thrushes
2 tbsp olive oil
1 lb/500 g puff pastry
  (see basic recipe)
3 juniper berries
6½ tbsp/100 ml
  Madeira wine
1 egg

Serves 6
Preparation time: 25 minutes
Cooking time: 40 minutes
Difficulty: ✶✶

1. Set aside enough foie gras to stuff the thrushes and combine the rest, by hand, with the sausage meat. Add salt and pepper to taste. Dice the prosciutto.

2. Pluck, gut, and clean the thrushes properly. Stuff them with a little foie gras, add salt and pepper. Pan-roast them in the oil. Let cool.

Twelve beautiful thrushes, flushed out of the bushes,
On a hill full of weeds in Lacaune, where the birds are second to none.
Pluck them and clean them, marinate them and season them.
Listen to your taste buds but always beware: When you cook the seasoned birds in earthenware
You're playing with fire! The aroma is likely to arouse your desire.
With the precious birds comes a special delight—A prosciutto whose flavor will light up the night.
With sausage and foie gras you've only to add a taste of Madeira to drive diners mad.
Or if not Madeira some other liquor that can soften the heart of the stoniest cur.
Take a pie plate all ready and prepped for a crust and fill it with everything with tenderness and trust
To the oven, consign it, with your eyes on the time
You'll wind up with a *Calais Thrushe* ever so fine.
Our wine expert suggests a red Gaillac (Jean Gros).

3. Roll out the pastry and press half of it into a deep pie pan. Leave some dough hanging over the edge. Spread the foie gras and sausage stuffing over the dough. Place the thrushes in a circle, their heads facing inward, on top of the stuffing.

4. Sprinkle the prosciutto over the thrushes, then add the juniper berries and Madeira. Beat the egg and brush it over the crust on the rim of the pie pan.

Pie

5. Roll out the remaining puff pastry and lay it over the top of the pie. Pinch the edges to seal.

6. Cut off the excess dough. Use a fork to mark the rim. Make a small hole in the middle. Brush the rest of the beaten egg over the top crust. Bake at 350 °F for 40 minutes.

Lacaune Blood

1. Carefully peel the blood sausage.

Ingredients:
1¼ lbs/600 g blood
   sausage
5 apples
1 tbsp/15 g butter
1 tbsp/15 ml oil
1 bunch of parsley
salt and pepper
To garnish: (optional)
cherry tomatoes
sprigs of rosemary

Serves 4
Preparation time: 15 minutes
Cooking time: 20 minutes
Difficulty: ✶

Our chef has recorded this original recipe expressly for this cookbook. It is bound to spice up the familiar and often repetitive repertoire of meat dishes. As a newcomer to world cuisine, this unusual dish offers an entirely new taste.

Blood sausage and apples are, in fact, classic elements of French cuisine. Tender sautéed apples, with a flavor that is at once acidic and sweet, are a perfect complement to the velvety texture of the sausage. And, of course, let us not forget the wonderful, healthful properties of the many different varieties of apples. You might also enjoy experimenting with the more exotic pineapple or the aristocratic pear either as substitutes for, or additions to, the apples.

The blood sausage can be cooked in a frying pan, as can the apples. The dish should be served very warm, though it can also be served as a leftover; just warm it up in the oven. The preparation is not time consuming. For those who like to eat well but have no time for complicated and involved recipes, this is a great solution.

Our chef's optional garnish of cherry tomato halves and rosemary make an eye-catching presentation.

To bring out the richness of this traditional blood sausage, serve a Chiroubles; it will add a fruity tang to the meal.

2. Cut the blood sausage in ⅜ in/1 cm slices.

3. Peel and core the apples. Cut them into slices just slightly thicker than the blood sausage.

4. Melt the butter in a pan and sauté the apples until tender. Salt lightly.

Sausage with Apples

5. In a separate pan, heat the oil and sauté the blood sausage. Add salt and pepper.

6. Chop the parsley and sprinkle it over the blood sausage. Arrange on a serving dish, alternating slices of blood sausage and apple. Garnish and serve.

Mushroom Cake

1. Peel the potatoes and boil them in salted water. When soft, drain and mash them.

Ingredients:
2.2 lbs/1 kg potatoes
6 egg yolks
4 tsp/20 g butter
7 oz/200 g porcini mushrooms
2 tbsp oil
6½ tbsp/100 ml heavy cream
6½ tbsp/100 ml milk
pinch of ground nutmeg
salt and pepper

Serves 6
Preparation time: 35 minutes
Cooking time: 45 minutes
Difficulty: ✴✴

2. While the mashed potatoes are still hot, add four of the egg yolks and the butter. Season with salt and pepper to taste. Dice the mushrooms.

The delicate taste and texture of the porcini mushroom makes it one of the most popular and highly regarded mushrooms. This method of preparation creates a delicious dish, which is also a piece of cake to make! It is mild and good, simple yet flavorful.

This "cake" is a variation of the more traditional quiche. It is, of course, possible to use other kinds of mushrooms or to add different herbs. The only *sine qua non* is that the savory filling be richer than the potato purée crust.

With respect to the black sauce, any dark sauce will do; you might try a civet, a Madeira sauce (see basic recipe), or a tomato-based sauce. Fry the mushrooms and let them cool enough that the potato paste is not melted by their heat. Also, the pie ring must stand firmly on the cookie sheet to prevent the paste from leaking out during baking.

This recipe, so rich in the produce of the earth, is a fine reflection of the hills of Lacaune. It is a heart-warming dish that will make any friend feel at home. In fact, it can be prepared the night before to give the cook more time with his or her dinner guests. Serve warm with a salad.

Our wine expert suggests a Saint-Émilion, in particular, a Château Trottevieille. The bouquet of such a great wine is often compared with the aroma of the porcini mushroom, and the combination of the two should infinitely enhance one's enjoyment.

3. Place a pie ring on a baking sheet. Using a pastry bag, squeeze circles of potato paste along the inside of the ring.

4. Heat the oil in a frying pan and brown the diced mushrooms. Add salt and pepper. Allow to cool, then spoon into the potato crust.

with Black Sauce

5. Combine the remaining egg yolks, the whole eggs, cream, milk, and a pinch of nutmeg. Stir vigorously.

6. Pour this mixture over the mushrooms and bake at 350 °F for 30 minutes. Remove the pie ring and set the cake on a serving dish accompanied by the black sauce of your choice.

Stewed Chanterelles

1. Prepare the pasta dough according to the basic recipe. Cook the noodles in a pot of boiling salted water until they are al dente.

Ingredients:
3½ oz/100 g fresh pasta (see basic recipe)
7 oz/200 g porcini
⅓ cup/80 g butter
2.2 lbs/1 kg chanterelles
several sprigs of parsley
1 clove of garlic
⅔ cup/150 ml heavy cream
salt and pepper

Serves 6
Preparation time: 20 minutes
Cooking time: 15 minutes
Difficulty: ✯

2. Carefully clean, peel, and then dice the porcini. Brown in a frying pan in half of the butter. Season with salt and pepper to taste.

There is nothing quite as enticing as the smell of stewed mushrooms; indeed, this whole dish is irresistible. There is also something very special about cooking a stew; sometimes it seems as if the preparation is more enjoyable than the actual eating. The chanterelles and the porcini mushrooms together make a very subtle, and priceless, alliance.

The garlic should barely cook before the cream is added. These two ingredients, combined, will set off the flavor of the mushrooms.

The pans in which the mushrooms are fried must be very hot. While cooking, the mushrooms should be stirred as little as possible. If mushrooms are overly manipulated, they do not brown properly.

There are no hidden tricks in this recipe; it only demands attention during the stewing stage. Our chef recommends sea salt for the water used to boil the pasta. Serve very warm. The fragrance of this dish will travel to every corner of every room and will tease the appetite of anyone within smelling distance. Vegetarians in particular will love this well-balanced meal.

Our wine expert suggests a dry Vouvray, which is a great French wine, at once sensuous and earthy.

3. Wash the chanterelles and cut each in half. Sauté in a separate pan in the remaining butter. Add salt and pepper.

4. Chop the parsley; mince the garlic. Combine the two kinds of mushrooms and add the parsley and garlic. Cook only briefly.

with Fresh Pasta

5. Pour in the cream and bring to a gentle boil.

6. Add the cooked pasta. Season to taste. Allow all the ingredients to settle and serve piping hot.

Potato Petals

1. Thinly slice the mushrooms and brown them in a pan with a little butter.

Ingredients:
3 medium-sized
   porcini mushrooms
1 clove of garlic,
   chopped
3 large potatoes
10 tbsp/150 g
   clarified butter
salt and pepper

Serves 3
Preparation time: 30 minutes
Cooking time: 20 minutes
Difficulty: ✶✶

2. Add salt, pepper, and chopped garlic. Remove the browned mushrooms and set them on a paper towel to soak up excess grease.

Our chef is a true poet. Like most great chefs, he loves flowers, and enjoys finding ways to make food, in this case potatoes, blossom. These paper-thin, translucent slices of potato encasing a single, succulent slice of porcini are truly a feast for the eyes as well as the palate.

To remove any humidity from the mushrooms, sauté them with a little garlic.

To obtain the thinnest possible slices of potatoes, use the thinnest position or blade available on your food processor. Do not forget to salt the slices. Salting serves two purposes here: It allows the potatoes to lose some of their starch, and it will help the two slices adhere more firmly. Let them rest a few minutes to soften after salting.

Clarify the butter over very low heat. Skim off the separated milk solids and retain the golden liquid which, like oil, will not burn, but will prevent any dark, bitter imperfections from forming on the potatoes. According to our wine expert, the "three magic words are: porcinis, potatoes, and Pomerol.

3. Peel the potatoes and, without washing them, cut them into very thin slices.

4. Place single potato slices on a cookie sheet and top each with one slice of porcini. Salt lightly.

with Porcini

5. Cover each mushroom with a second slice of potato. Gently press the edges of the potato slices together so that they will adhere.

6. Fry the potato petals in the clarified butter, flipping them from time to time. Salt and serve warm.

Warm Oysters

Ingredients:
- 3½ oz/100 g prosciutto
- 1 bunch of parsley
- 3½ oz/100 g porcini
- 2 shallots
- 2 cloves of garlic
- 12 oysters
- ¾ cup/200 ml white wine
- 1 cup/250 ml crème fraîche
- 4 egg yolks
- salt and pepper

1. Finely chop the prosciutto, parsley, porcini, and shallots, and set each aside. Mince the garlic and reserve for the final step.

Serves 2
Preparation time: 40 minutes
Cooking time: 10 minutes
Difficulty: ✱✱

2. Shuck the oysters and remove from their shells. Bring a pot of water to a boil, add the wine and blanche the oysters in it for just 1 minute. Do not overcook.

The love of oysters, so common today, is hardly new. The ancient Greeks had cultivated them, and the Celts and Romans were also known to be avid consumers of this mollusk. In the Middle Ages, oysters were sold with or without their shell. Louis XIV's physician reportedly wanted the king to avoid them, and failing that, insisted at the very least that they be cooked for the monarch.

This is a perfect appetizer and it can easily be transformed into an entrée—simply reduce the number of oysters served per person, accompanied by a lobster mousse.

Mussels could also be substituted for the oysters; the former are easier to find, though generally less tasty. Of the several varieties of French oysters, our chef recommends the Marennes oysters or Brittany oysters. Their cooking time is very short; they should be blanched for only one minute and must be removed from the boiling water very quickly or they will turn rubbery and ruin the whole dish.

For the palate inclined toward the spicy, try adding some cayenne pepper to the sauce. This winter dish, elegant and refined, should be served warm and fresh from the oven. It is suitable for any important meal.

White Graves, like oysters, have that wonderful aftertaste reminiscent of the sea. Our wine expert suggests a Château Carbonnieux.

3. In a frying pan, brown the shallots. Add the prosciutto, parsley and mushrooms. Sauté until all ingredients have browned nicely. Add salt and pepper. Place a spoonful of the browned mixture in each oyster shell.

4. Lay a poached oyster over the filling in each shell.

à la Landes

5. Heat ¾ of the crème fraîche and reduce for a few minutes. Combine the egg yolks with the remaining crème fraîche and pour into the simmering crème fraîche while beating vigorously. Do not allow this mixture to boil.

6. Season sauce to taste. Sprinkle each oyster with chopped garlic and cover with sauce. Broil a few minutes until the sauce is browned and bubbly. Serve warm.

Duck Foie Gras

Ingredients:
1 lb/500 g foie gras
a pinch of sugar
3 carrots
2 onions
1 cluster of grapes
1 cup/250 ml white
    wine
3½ tbsp/50 ml
    muscatel wine
salt and pepper

Serves 6
Preparation time: 25 minutes
Cooking time: 25 minutes
Difficulty: ★★

1. If you are using a fresh foie gras, remove the central nerve from each lobe; also remove the gall bladder. Add salt and pepper and a dash of sugar.

2. Peel the carrots and onions. Slice both thinly and combine in a pot. Place the foie gras on top of the vegetables. Cover and cook over low heat for 20 minutes, stirring occasionally.

Foie gras, the crown jewel of French gastronomy, consists of the liver of a duck or goose which has been specially fed and fattened. The Romans already practiced this method of preparing duck and goose livers, although the animals were fed figs rather than corn, as is customary today.

The reputation of goose foie gras, with its incredibly delicate taste, is totally secure. Duck foie gras, on the other hand, still has room for improvement. Though it collapses more often when cooked, its stronger taste lingers longer on the tongue.

Our chef suggests a very unripe grape and warns against using raisins. Verjuice would be an excellent addition; its acidity highlights the sumptuousness of the foie gras.

If you have the opportunity to select a fresh foie gras, look for one that is supple but not soft, with few visible nerves. These must be trimmed before cooking, as they otherwise shrink and ruin the dish. Also, foie gras loses less fat and water during cooking once they are removed. Adding a pinch of sugar balances the foie gras' slight bitterness. Finally, handle foie gras as little as possible to minimize collapsing during cooking.

As an appetizer for a festive meal at Christmas time or New Year's, this prestigious dish will introduce your guest to the delights of tradition. This dish cannot be reheated.

Our wine expert feels that the bouquet of grapes, whether on a plate or in a glass, is in perfect harmony with the discrete bitterness of the foie gras. He therefore recommends a Meursault Charmes.

3. Peel each grape and poach lightly in the white wine; set the grapes aside.

4. Remove the foie gras from the pot. Pour the wine used to poach the grapes over the vegetables. Lightly salt and pepper.

with Grapes

5. Stir this mixture well. Bring it to a boil before pouring it through a strainer. Bring the liquid to a boil once more. Add the whole grapes and the muscatel wine.

6. Slice the foie gras and arrange the slices on a serving dish. Spoon the sauce over the foie gras. Serve warm garnished with the grapes.

Veal Kidneys

1. Rinse the mint leaves and chop them well. Peel and chop the shallots.

Ingredients:
15 mint leaves
3 shallots
2 veal kidneys
3½ tbsp/50 ml oil
4 tbsp/60 g butter
¾ cup/200 ml white wine
¾ cup/200 ml crème fraîche
salt and pepper

Serves 4
Preparation time: 20 minutes
Cooking time: 25 minutes
Difficulty: ✲

2. Cut the kidneys into large chunks. Sear them in a pan with the oil and a teaspoon of butter. Add salt and pepper.

The kidney is a red organ meat, light and delicate. Veal kidneys are often sold encased in a thin, transparent film that has to be removed, along with any nerves and the thick layer of protective fat. Lamb kidneys are also acceptable, but our chef prefers the slightly more delicate taste of veal. Like other red organ meats, kidneys are rich in iron and therefore often recommended to fight fatigue.

The kidneys should be seared very quickly but remain somewhat pink. If you prefer them well done, cut thin slices into them so they cook thoroughly in less time, before they have a chance to become dry and rubbery.

It is somewhat unusual to see mint in a recipe of this type; mint lends its unique taste and fresh, peppery aroma. While kidneys cooked with champagne or port are a guaranteed success, it is exciting to try new flavors and variations of classic dishes.

This is a simple dish; only the actual cooking will demand your full attention. The kidneys must be served warm, immediately after being cooked. They cannot be warmed up, so take advantage of them right away. They are nicely complimented by potatoes or other vegetables. A delicate and discretely refined dish, this is an ideal meal for two.

We suggest a Gewurztraminer. Our wine expert tells us that this great Alsacian wine is seductive and will bring out the mint overtones of this appetizer.

3. Combine the shallots in a pot with the wine and crème fraîche and cook over low heat. Add salt and pepper.

4. After about 5 minutes, add the seared kidneys. Cook for 10 minutes. Remove the kidneys and place them on a serving platter. Add the chopped mint to the sauce. Whip with half the remaining butter.

with Fresh Mint

5. Mix with an electric mixer until the mint is thoroughly pulverized. Blend in the remaining butter.

6. Pour the sauce over the kidneys. Serve warm with potatoes.

Eel Pâté

1. Skin and fillet the eel (see basic recipe).

Ingredients:
1 1½ lb/700-800 g eel
3 shallots
1 sprig of thyme
2 laurel leaves
3/4 cup/200 ml dry
   white wine
1 lb/500 g whiting
   fillet
1 egg white
1 cup/250 ml crème
   fraîche
3½ tbsp/50 g butter
1 lb/500 g puff pastry
   (see basic recipe)
1 small bunch of
   chives
salt and pepper

Serves 6
Preparation time: 55 minutes
Marinating time: 12 hours
Cooking time: 45 minutes
Difficulty: ✶✶

This classic example of a country pâté, which is actually the French word for pie, contains ingredients from the Aquitaine region in southwest France and is reminiscent of the swampy lands of Sologne. Unlike other pâtés, however, this one is served warm.

If you are a purist who would rather not mix a saltwater and a freshwater fish, pike may be substituted for the whiting without any loss in taste or quality. Another exciting variation would be to add a truffle to the filling.

A few pointers from our chef: The eel must marinate for at least twelve hours, or overnight. Wrap the fish roll very tightly in plastic wrap, or buttered wax paper, and drain the fish roll as soon as it has cooked, rather than letting it cool in the cooking liquid. It is important for the pastry to be cold when it is wrapped around the roll of fish. Finally, once the sauce has been whipped, do not allow it to boil.

Puff pastry will absorb humidity or liquid, and its texture suffers from being reheated. The filling alone, however, can be refrigerated for several days.

To accompany the thick, strong meat of the eel, which is very difficult to match with an appropriate wine, our wine expert recommends a white Cheverny.

2. Peel and finely chop the shallots. In a large pot, sprinkle the shallots over the eel. Add the thyme, laurel and salt and pepper. Pour in the wine and let the mixture marinate in the refrigerator for 12 hours or more.

3. Cut up the whiting fillets and combine with the egg white. Add salt and pepper and blend in a food processor. Add ⅔ of the crème fraîche. Blend again until the mixture becomes a smooth mousse.

4. Remove the eel fillets from the marinade. Place an eel fillet on a large piece of plastic wrap. Spread some of the mousse over it. Continue to layer, ending with a fillet. Roll up the plastic wrap tightly to make a sausage-like form.

à la Sologne

5. Place the fish roll in a loaf pan and pour the marinade over it. Add water to cover. Bake in a 300 °F oven until the fish is cooked. Drain the liquid and let the fish roll cool. Prepare and roll out the puff pastry.

6. Unwrap the fish roll and set it on a sheet of pastry. Cover with another layer of pastry, seal edges, and bake 30 minutes at 350 °F. For the sauce, reduce the marinade by ¼, add the remaining crème fraîche, thicken and strain. Just before serving, whip in the butter. Stir chopped chives into the sauce. Serve warm.

Snail and

1. Peel, seed and dice the tomatoes. Chop the garlic, parsley, and shallot. Cut up the snails.

Ingredients:

2 tomatoes
3 cloves of garlic
1 bunch of parsley
1 shallot
48 snails
3½ tbsp/50 g butter
5½ oz/150 g noodle dough
1 egg
2½ cups/600 ml chicken stock
6½ tbsp/100 ml crème fraîche
2 egg yolks
6½ tbsp/100 ml olive oil
salt and pepper

Serves 4
Preparation time: 1 hour 10 minutes
Cooking time: 25 minutes
Difficulty: ✶✶✶

2. Let the shallot and ⅓ of the garlic sweat in a frying pan with 1 tbsp butter. Stir in the snails and cook over low heat until the moisture has evaporated. Sprinkle with salt and pepper. Add the parsley and tomatoes, and again cook until quite dry. Let cool.

These raviolis, a hallmark of traditional cuisine from Corsica, Nice, and the southern region of France in general, are first cousins of Italian raviolis.

Filled with petit-gris snails, these baby turnovers are a real treasure! This is a serious appetizer that will dignify any meal. Its preparation is time-intensive, there are no shortcuts, and several of the steps are tricky, but the delectible end result is well worth the trouble and time.

In order to close each ravioli, do not overstuff them with filling. Press firmly on the edges until they adhere to each other; they will finish sealing themselves as they cook. Pat them dry with a paper towel before serving to eliminate any excess fat.

For visual appeal, cut a peeled and seeded tomato into small triangles. The red on white will brighten up the entire table.

Try a Condrieu with these delicate raviolis. It is a wonderful white wine, the best wine to serve with garlic, though it has unfortunately become difficult to find.

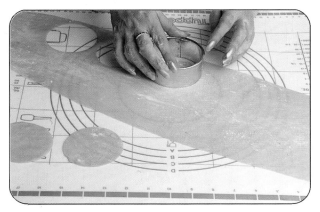

3. Roll out the pasta dough very thinly. Cut out circles approximately 2 in/5-6 cm in diameter.

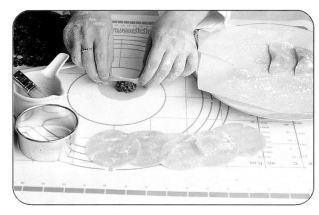

4. Place a spoonful of the cooled filling onto each pasta circle. Gently brush the edges of the circle with beaten egg. Fold the raviolis in half, turnover-style.

Garlic Ravioli

5. In a saucepan, reduce the chicken stock to half its original volume. Add the crème fraîche and allow to thicken. In a separate bowl, combine two egg yolks and the rest of the garlic. Slowly beat in the olive oil so the mixture rises; add to the sauce. Pass the sauce through a strainer. Do not let it boil.

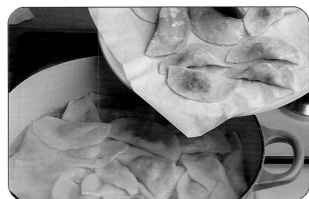

6. Boil the raviolis in salted water for 5 minutes. Drain and place on warm dishes. Cover them with the sauce and serve.

Sardine

1. Roll out the pastry and cut out a circle with a diameter of 6 in/15 cm. Prick it with a fork and bake at 350 °F until golden brown. Crumble the bread in a food processor.

2. Chop the shallots and garlic and sauté in the butter without letting them brown. Combine them with the bread crumbs, crème fraîche, basil, parsley, and egg yolk. Salt and pepper to taste. Set aside.

3. Clean and fillet the sardines (see basic recipe), add salt and pepper. Set a flan ring on a buttered baking sheet. Arrange the sardines in the circle, folded in half with the skin on the outside and the fold toward the outer edge of the ring.

Ingredients:
5¼ oz/150 g puff pastry
  (see basic recipe)
3 slices of white bread
¾ oz/20 g shallots
½ clove of garlic
1 tbsp/15 g butter
1 tbsp crème fraîche
5 basil leaves, chopped
1 tbsp parsley, chopped
1 egg yolk
18 sardines
6 baby onions
1 tbsp/15 ml olive oil
For the sauce:
4 tomatoes
½ clove of garlic
5 anchovy fillets
½ cup/120 g butter
salt and pepper

Serves 4
Preparation time: 40 minutes
Cooking time: 20 minutes
Difficulty: ✶

Sardines, little cousins of the herring, are rich in phosphorus and calcium and have been popular for centuries. Greeks fished them off the coast of Sardinia, from which they derived their name. The sardine is primarily in season in the spring but is also available during summer months.

To save time, you may choose to make a short pastry without sugar, instead of the more time-consuming puff pastry. Prick the pastry with a fork before baking so that it does not rise excessively.

The julienne onions, lightly browned in olive oil and slightly crisp, add a rich, deep flavor to the composition. The sauce should not be too thick; it can be diluted with water if necessary.

Our chef suggests preparing individual pies, each about 3¼ inches (8 cm) in diameter, or try making it with mackerel. This crisp fish pie is perfect for summer meals at the beach. As for wine, our expert suggests a Bellet (Château de Crémat). This little vineyard, with its grapes facing the bay of Anges, produces tender yet lively wines.

4. Cover the sardines with the bread mixture. Bake at 450 °F for 5 minutes.

Pie

5. Prepare the sauce: Seed and dice the tomatoes. Stir them over low heat with the chopped garlic and anchovy fillets for 5 minutes. Add a little water. Blend in a food processor, then strain. Whip in the butter and adjust the seasoning. Set aside, keeping warm, but do not allow to boil.

6. Peel and julienne the onions, then sauté in the olive oil without letting them brown. Spread the onions on top of the baked pastry and use a large spatula to set the sardine pie on top of the onions. Serve warm with the tomato sauce.

Garenne

1. Clean and bone the rabbit. Peel and thinly slice the shallots and carrot.

2. In a bowl, marinate the rabbit with the 3 herbs and the sliced shallots and carrot. Salt and pepper lightly. Add the wine and cognac.

3. Let the rabbit marinate for 48 hours. Drain the rabbit, reserving the marinade, and grind the meat.

Ingredients:
1 rabbit, approx. 2.2
   lbs/1 kg
2 shallots
1 carrot
1 bunch of parsley
   stems
1 tsp chopped thyme
1 tsp chopped laurel
1¼ cups/300 ml wine,
   e.g. Côtes du Rhône
3½ tbsp/50 ml cognac
3 eggs
1 tsp *quatre épices*
12¼ oz/350 g puff
   pastry (see basic
   recipe)
1 tbsp/15 ml crème
   fraîche
salt and pepper

Serves 6
Preparation time: 50 minutes
Cooking time: 40 minutes
Difficulty: ✶✶

The Garenne rabbit is a wild rabbit that enjoys its freedom. It eats only wild, natural greens, and these give its meat a very delicate flavor.

If you are in the unique position of having a freshly killed rabbit from a hunting trip, you will have to skin and clean it. To remove the skin without damaging the meat, cut the skin down the middle, while making a circle from the stomach to the back, and pull. The fur comes off like a glove.

Do not use the front paws in this recipe; they are too tough. They can, however, always be saved for flavoring a sauce.

Our chef suggests a good, strong wine for the marinade, such as a Côtes du Rhône. The marinade can be reduced by half its volume to cut the acidity introduced by the wine. The vegetables in this recipe add flavor to the marinade, but do not actually appear in the stuffing. Be sure to save a few tablespoons of the marinade for basting the stuffing, which will keep it moist.

Another element of the special taste of this pie is *quatre épices*, a combination of ground nutmeg, ginger, cinnamon, and cloves that adds a nice twist to the filling.

For an extra special meal, prepare individual pies and serve them with a festive salad.

Our wine expert recommends a Chablis Fourchaumes. The white meat of the rabbit goes well with a tender and elegant white wine.

4. Add 2 eggs to the ground rabbit meat, stir, and adjust the seasoning if necessary. Add the quatre épices. Roll out the puff pastry and cut out 2 circles. Ease one in a buttered pie pan.

Rabbit Pie

5. Stir the crème fraîche into the rabbit mixture and spoon the filling into the pie crust.

6. Separate the remaining egg and use the yolk to moisten the pastry along the edge of the pan so the top crust will adhere to the bottom one. Lay the top layer over the pie and seal the edges. Trim off any excess dough. Bake at 350 °F for 40 minutes.

The Drunkard's

1. Dissolve the bouillon in 6½ tbsp/100 ml boiling water. In a separate pan, melt the butter and brown the chopped shallots. Add the wine. Lightly salt and pepper. Stir in the thyme and laurel.

Ingredients:

1 cube veal bouillon
6½ tbsp/100 g butter
4 shallots, chopped
3 cups/750 ml red wine
1 sprig of thyme
2-3 laurel leaves
5 andouillette sausages
6½ tbsp/100 ml heavy cream
salt and pepper

Serves 5
Preparation time: 10 minutes
Cooking time: 35 minutes
Difficulty: ✳

2. After about 20 minutes, pour in the bouillon and let simmer for another 15 minutes. Stir occasionally.

The andouillette, a bold and flavorful sausage made from chitterling and tripe, naturally has a large following among chitterling lovers. In earlier butcher traditions, the tripe was cut lengthwise. Today, the tripe is usually cut in squares. Historically, the Normandy andouillette is accompanied by apples, but in this recipe our chef offers an original wine-based alternative.

The andouillette must be well browned on all sides, but take care during cooking not to let the pan overheat or the sausages will burst. They should cook over moderate heat. Our chef suggests a Côtes du Rhône for the sauce; it is a powerful wine that will add body and fragrance. To purge the sauce of the bitter taste introduced by the wine, let it simmer for a relatively long time and reduce it with the shallots. For a smoother sauce, the shallots can be removed before serving.

This appetizer can be accompanied by mashed or sautéed potatoes, but if you'd like to try something less commonplace, try red cabbage with apples. You won't be disappointed!

A little more tender and sweet than its Hermitage cousin, a Crozes is, in our wine expert's opinion, the ideal wine for this Drunkard's Andouillete.

3. In a nonstick pan, brown the andouillettes, turning them often. Very lightly salt and pepper them.

4. Set the andouillettes aside, but keep warm. Deglaze the pan with some of the sauce and reduce for a few minutes.

Andouillette

5. Pour in the rest of the sauce and stir in the cream. Simmer gently and allow to thicken. Adjust the seasoning if necessary.

6. Strain the sauce. Pour it on a platter and arrange the andouillettes on top. Serve warm.

Cabbage

1. *Thinly slice the cabbage, then blanch it in lightly salted boiling water. Take care not to overcook.*

Ingredients:
1 white cabbage
3½ oz/100 g Swiss cheese
2 cups/500 ml heavy cream
salt and pepper

Serves 4
Preparation time: 15 minutes
Cooking time: 15 minutes
Difficulty: ✷

2. *Grate the cheese.*

On a gastronomical trip through the beautiful French countryside, you may wend your way toward the Auge region of Normandy, where you will leave behind the chill of winter and find yourself warmed up by dishes such as this.

Of all fresh vegetables, the leafy vegetables are the easiest to find throughout the year; they are rich in vitamins A and C, in iron and calcium, and in fiber.

The core and stiffer outer leaves of the cabbage should be removed. The cabbage should be sliced thinly to allow rapid cooking. If the cabbage remains slightly crunchy, it will retain more of its nutritional value. To halt cooking after blanching, rinse the cabbage in cold water. This is an essential step and should not be omitted.

For variety and novelty, try red cabbage instead of white, or even thinly sliced zucchini. If you do choose zucchini, be sure to steam it first.

This gratin should be served warm and will go nicely with a meal of game or pork served with a red wine-based sauce.

For this dish, you will want to choose a wine to suit the meat, though you might show your adventurous spirit with a daring red Bourgueil or white Sancerre regardless of the main course.

3. *Drain the cabbage and run under cold water to stop it from cooking in its own heat. Spread the cabbage in a greased baking dish.*

4. *Sprinkle the cheese over the cabbage.*

au Gratin

5. Add salt and pepper to the cream and whip briefly.

6. Pour the cream over the cabbage. Bake at 425 °F for 15 minutes, then broil a few minutes to brown. Serve piping hot.

Minced Endive with

1. Cut the bacon into thin strips.

Ingredients:
7 oz/200 g bacon
4 endives
3½ tbsp/50 g butter
3½ tbsp/50 ml vinegar
3½ tbsp/50 ml crème
   fraîche
4 tomatoes
salt and pepper

Serves 4
Preparation time: 10 minutes
Cooking time: 15 minutes
Difficulty: ✻

2. Remove the head of each endive. Separate the leaves, leaving a few whole for the garnish. Braise these in hot butter for a few seconds, lightly salt and pepper, and set aside. Thinly slice the rest of the endive and sweat in butter.

Endive was discovered not so long ago, in 1850, by a farmer from Brussels who discovered that in a warm, dark environment wild chicory grew long, yellowish, edible leaves. He began to cultivate them, and a Belgian botanist perfected the process.

This winter vegetable is ideal: It is easily digestible, low in calories, and rich in potassium, as well as in vitamins C, B1, B2, K and provitamin A.

Our chef suggests squeezing a little lemon juice on the endive leaves before cutting them to help them stay white. This will also reduce their bitterness and keep them crisp.

To keep the tomatoes from blanching, brown them in a very small quantity of butter.

If your guests are not bacon lovers, you can try replacing the bacon with a cured beef.

This dish must be served hot; it cannot be rewarmed. The endive leaves will not tolerate being cooked twice.

We suggest a dry Vouvray (Domaine G. Huet); it will help you find a comforting middle ground between the food and spirits.

3. Add the bacon to the endive. Brown lightly over low heat.

4. Deglaze the pan with the vinegar. Lightly salt and pepper.

Tomato and Bacon

5. Stir in the crème fraîche and let the mixture thicken over low heat.

6. Peel, seed, and dice the tomatoes. Brown them very lightly in a little butter. Add salt and pepper. Place the bacon and endive mixture in the center of a serving plate, surrounded by the whole endive leaves filled with tomatoes.

Jumbo Shrimp

1. Peel the shrimp and remove the heads. Brown them in a frying pan with the melted butter. Lightly salt and pepper. When done, set aside. Soak the morels in a bowl of water.

Ingredients:
20 jumbo shrimp
2 tbsp/30 g butter
3½ oz/100 g freeze-
    dried morels
2 shallots
3½ tbsp/50 ml cognac
¾ cup/200 ml heavy
    cream
4 tomatoes
salt and pepper

Serves 4
Preparation time: 25 minutes
Cooking time: 15 minutes
Difficulty: ✶✶

Ordinarily it is terribly difficult to prepare an extraordinary meal in a very short time! Yet here is a recipe of such beauty, simplicity, finesse, and speed that it defies definition as anything but a work of art.

It is also a recipe that is easily modified. One can use regular shrimp or some other shellfish. The morels are strong enough to hold their own with many different flavors.

Tomatoes are a nutritional wonder: According to one dietician, a mere 3 1/2 ounces of tomatoes can provide 13% of the recommended daily allowance of vitamin A, 5% of folic acid, 8% of vitamin B1, and 33% of vitamin C. Tomatoes are energizing, revitalizing and refreshing.

Our chef suggests that you not remove too much pulp when hollowing out the tomatoes; keep in mind that they need to remain firm enough to stand upright.

This meal should be served warm and does not lend itself to reheating.

The delicate daring of a chablis is perfectly suited to this impish dish. Try a Chablis (Domaine Laroche).

2. Peel and chop the shallots and sauté them in the same pan used for the shrimp. Do not let the shallots brown.

3. Remove the stems from the morels and gently wash under running water. Drain thoroughly and add to the shallots.

4. Remove the morels and shallots from the pan and pour out any butter. Return the morels and shallots to the pan and flambé them with the cognac.

in Morel Sauce

5. Add the cream and let simmer for 4 to 5 minutes over low heat. Adjust the seasoning and set aside.

6. Cut the tops off the tomatoes and hollow them out. Put them in the oven for about 10 minutes. Stand the tomatoes on a platter and arrange the shrimp inside them. Serve with the morels and cream sauce.

Sautéed Foie

1. Peel and core the apples. Cut them in half and then slice them.

Ingredients:
3 apples
4 tsp/20 g butter
6 thick slices of duck
   foie gras
2 tbsp/30 ml honey
6½ tbsp/100 ml
   vinegar
salt and pepper

Serves 3
Preparation time: 15 minutes
Cooking time: 15 minutes
Difficulty: ✶

2. Brown the apple slices in a frying pan with the butter.

It has been proven that foie gras dates back at least to the Roman times. Culinary historians believe that the process is even older, and that the Romans may have adapted the idea from the Greeks or the Phoenicians. To fatten up goose or duck livers for foie gras, animals were blinded so that they could not tell day from night, and spent all their time eating.

When choosing a foie gras, a good rule of thumb is to be sure that it is firm and elastic. If it is too soft, it will collapse quickly when cooked. Bear in mind, moreover, that duck foie gras collapses faster than goose foie gras. It should therefore be kept in the refrigerator until it is sliced.

The pan used for searing should be very hot so that the foie gras slices cook quickly.

You may use any kind of apple, though the Golden Delicious apple keeps its shape and consistency best. Giant raisins or dried turnips also make excellent accompaniments to foie gras.

This dish should be served immediately after it is cooked, and cannot be warmed up.

Either a red or a white wine will do well here. The only direction offered by our wine expert is to avoid wine with a high tannin content. You might wish to try a white Saint-Joseph or a Volnay Caillerets.

3. Cut the foie gras into slices approximately ¼ in/5 mm thick. Salt and pepper.

4. In a very hot nonstick pan, sear the foie gras slices, turning them occasionally. Five minutes should be sufficient.

Gras with Apples

5. Blend the honey and vinegar. Beat thoroughly.

6. Lay the apples in a ring on a serving platter. Deglaze the foie gras pan with the vinegar/honey mixture. Place the foie gras slices on the apples. Let the sauce reduce for a minute or two. Pour the sauce over the foie gras and apples and serve piping hot.

Potatoes au Gratin

1. Peel the potatoes and slice them very thinly in a food processor. Lightly steam them or cook briefly in boiling water.

Ingredients:
2.2 lbs/1 kg potatoes
1 cup/220 g creme
  fraîche
3 1/2 oz/100 g
  Laguiole cheese
1 pinch of ground
  nutmeg
4 cloves of garlic
salt and pepper

Serves 6
Preparation time: 20 minutes
Cooking time: 50 minutes
Difficulty: ✶

2. Once steamed or boiled, remove the potatoes with a strainer and put them in a mixing bowl.

The *Laguiole Aubrac* or *Fourme de Laguiole* (pronounced "layole") is a cow's milk cheese made in the Aubrac region, protected by an *appellation controlée*, with a soft, non-baked flavor and a traditional gray rind.

If you should ever find yourself in the vicinity of Rouregue, be sure to seek out and explore one of the *burons*, the cottages in which this cheese is traditionally made.

Laguiole is at its peak between the months of July and March.

The potatoes should be rinsed well to remove their surface starch.

This traditional recipe is easily reheated. Served warm, it is a perfect accompaniment for meat or poultry.

Your wine should be chosen to complement the meat with which you serve this potato gratin. Still, to pay respect to this recipe's rustic side, try a white Quincy or a red Cahors.

3. Stir in the crème fraîche. Add salt and pepper and mix well.

4. Grate the cheese and stir half of it into the potatoes. Add a pinch of nutmeg.

with Laguiole

5. Chop the garlic finely and mix in; carefully combine until all ingredients are well-blended.

6. Butter a baking dish. Turn the potatoes into the dish and sprinkle the remaining cheese on the top. Bake at 300 °F for 45 minutes. Serve piping hot.

Langoustine Papillotes

1. Peel the carrots and leeks. Slice them à la julienne. Poach each vegetable in a separate pot of gently boiling water.

Ingredients:
2 carrots
2 leeks
16 langoustines
4 oz/120 g duck foie gras
1 tbsp dried tarragon
salt and pepper

Serves 4
Preparation time: 20 minutes
Cooking time: 15 minutes
Difficulty: ✶✶

2. Remove the tail meat from the langoustine shells; save the meat and the shells.

In the cooking method used here, *papillote*—the term is probably derived from the French word for butterfly, *papillon*—each individual langoustine is delicately wrapped in aluminum foil. The effect is surprising and charming.

Do not be deceived by the claws on the langoustines. Despite their size, they contain very little meat. The real treasure of the langoustine lies in its tail.

Use fresh tarragon and sprinkle it on each langoustine tail before baking. For the langoustines to turn out perfectly, each one must be sealed as tightly as possible inside the foil. Also try to incorporate some air into each pocket. While baking, the heated air will puff up the foil pouch and the result will be all the more attractive.

If you should tire of langoustines, scallops could be substituted.

These papillotes cannot be reheated and must be served very warm. They are delightful served with pasta, with some lemon wedges on hand for those who like lemon juice with their shellfish.

Our wine expert would invite you to discover one of the best wines in France, known for its many nuances: a Savennière, Clos de la Coulée-de-Serrant.

3. Cut 4 slices of foie gras.

4. For each serving, lay out a sheet of aluminum foil. Set 4 langoustine tails on their sides. At the center of the 4 tails, place a serving of carrots and leeks, and sprinkle a pinch of tarragon over both.

with Foie Gras

5. Place a slice of foie gras over the vegetables.

6. Fold the sides of the foil over the contents and seal tightly. Bake at 400 °F for 10 minutes.

Seafood

1. *Peel and finely chop the shallots. Combine half of them with ¼ cup wine; divide evenly between 2 pots and simmer. Steam the mussels and clams in another pot. Once opened, remove meat from shells; reserve. Shuck the oysters and remove from their shells.*

2. *In a pan, brown the remaining shallots with 1 tbsp of butter. Chop the oysters, add to the pan along with the chopped parsley, and brown for a few seconds.*

Ingredients:
4 shallots
1 cup white wine
2 cups mussels
2 cups clams
4 oysters
1 bunch of parsley
pasta dough (see
    basic recipe) or
    Chinese dumpling
    wrappers
6½ tbsp/100 g butter
6½ tbsp/100 ml
    crème fraîche
4 langoustine tails
1 leek
olive oil
salt and pepper

Serves 4
Preparation time: 25 minutes
Cooking time: 30 minutes
Difficulty: ✳✳✳

These delightful little pasta pouches are a creative composition of complex and yet similar flavors.

Since the preparation of pasta dough is a time-consuming enterprise, our chef suggests buying premade Chinese dumpling wrappers. They can be found in Asian markets or in the specialty aisle of any large supermarket.

Any one of the seafood ingredients can be substituted or replaced with another.

The chopped oysters should only brown for a few seconds or they will become tough. The pasta suffers from the same problem, since it tears easily and the filling is fairly heavy. The trickiest part of this recipe is handling the pasta. One important tip: Immerse the ravioli in boiling water for a few seconds, then plunge them into cold water to stop the pasta from absorbing and retaining water (which would make them difficult to handle). The pouches are then ready to be bathed in creamy sauce and enjoyed.

The attractive leek ribbon used to tie these delicate pockets will make your raviolis the highlight of your party.

The shellfish are wonderfully complimented by a Muscadet sur lie.

3. *Strain the liquid in which the mussels and clams were steamed. Bring to a boil and reduce its volume by half. Add the crème fraîche and again reduce until the mixture is homogeneous. Prepare the noodle dough according to the basic recipe, if you choose to make your own.*

4. *Once the pasta has been well-kneaded and allowed to rest, roll it out very thinly and cut circles about 5 in/12 cm in diameter. Quickly poach each circle, cool, drain well, and set aside on a dish towel.*

Ravioli

5. Slice the leek lengthwise and blanch the long strips. Place 1 tbsp of the oyster meat on each circle. Then add mussels, clams, and a langoustine tail. Close the pouch and tie it with a strip of blanched leek.

6. Gently place the raviolis in a baking dish and cover with the sauce. Bake at 350 °F for a few minutes. Remove the raviolis from the sauce and arrange on serving dishes. Strain the sauce, enrich it with butter, and pour over the raviolis just before serving.

Sautéed Chanterelles

1. Clean the chanterelles. Blend half in a food processor and add trimmings from the non-flowering ends of the zucchini. Soak the bread in a little cream, then add. Salt and pepper. Add the egg and cream by spoonfuls, puréeing until smooth but not too liquid.

2. Bring a pot of lightly salted water to a boil. Blanch the zucchini for one minute. Drain and plunge in cold water to stop the cooking process.

Ingredients:
1 lb/500 g chanterelle mushrooms
12 zucchinis with flowers attached
2 slices of white bread
6½ tbsp/100 ml heavy cream
1 egg
3 cloves of garlic
1 bunch of parsley
3 shallots
6½ tbsp/100 ml butter
juice of 1 lemon
10 basil leaves, sliced
salt and pepper

Serves 4
Preparation time: 25 minutes
Cooking time: 20 minutes
Difficulty: ✶✶

Zucchini in bloom has a delicate and light flavor; the lively orange blossoms will bring springtime to any table.

Pour the cream in a little at a time. The stuffing should not be too runny, though it should resemble a purée.

Blow gently into the zuccini flower to spread it to give you room for the stuffing without damaging the vegetable.

Use a paper towel to remove excess fat from the mushrooms.

If you are serving the zucchini for a special occasion, consider using truffles as a final touch. Simply inserting thin slices of truffle into each zucchini blossom will lend this appetizer a touch of class and elegance.

Zucchini and white Bellet are neighbors. They will most certainly be good company.

3. Gently open the zucchini blossoms. Fill a pastry bag with the chanterelle purée and fill each flower, then sprinkle with salt. Chop the garlic and parsley.

4. Chop 1 shallot and brown it in a pan with some oil. Add the chanterelles reserved from Step 1 and brown over low heat. Stir in the chopped garlic and parsley.

with Flowering Zucchini

5. Steam the filled zucchini for approximately 15 minutes. Chop the remaining shallots and brown them. Add the lemon juice, then whisk in the butter.

6. Pour the shallots and butter through a strainer to remove the shallots. Add the basil leaves and let them flavor the butter. Arrange the zucchini on a serving dish. Add the sautéed chanterelles and cover with the butter sauce.

Truffle

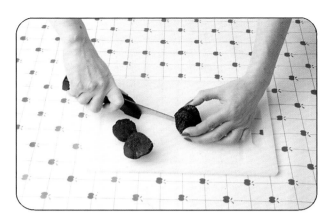

1. Cut the truffles in half and set aside.

Ingredients:
2 large fresh truffles
10½ oz/300 g puff pastry (see basic recipe)
5¼ oz/150 g foie gras
6½ tbsp/50 g flour
1 egg, beaten
salt and pepper
Madeira sauce (see basic recipe)

Serves 4
Preparation time: 20 minutes
Cooking time: 25 minutes
Difficulty: ✳

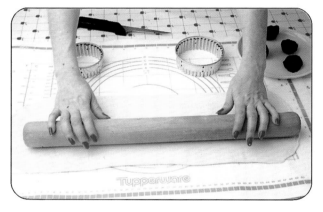

2. Prepare the puff pastry according to the basic recipe, then roll it out very thinly.

These delicious pouches would be a stupendous culinary Christmas present during the holiday season. The recipe requires only a little extra attention and care.

Beginners are recommended to either buy the puff pastry, or at least prepare it well in advance. The pastry should be very thinly rolled out so that it does not rise and become thick when baked. The edges of the pastry should be moistened with a beaten egg to help them adhere to each other.

The foie gras needs to be cooked in a nonstick pan with no butter or oil, over very high heat. But beware, it melts very quickly, so do not let it out of your sight.

Use the tip of a knife to draw out the sauce and decorate the serving platter.

Our wine expert suggests a Clos-Vougeot. This wine will add pleasure to the appetizer and will bring out the best in the majestic truffle and aristocratic foie gras.

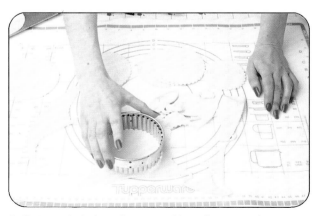

3. Cut out 4 circles of pastry with a diameter of approximately 2 in/5 cm, and 4 additional circles of about 2¾ in/7cm.

4. Slice the foie gras into 4 pieces and coat each with flour. Season lightly with salt and pepper.

Pouches

5. Place one slice of foie gras on each of the smaller pastry circles.

6. Top each with half a truffle. Brush the edges of the pastry with beaten egg and cover with the larger circles. Press the edges of each circle to seal. Bake at 350 °F for 20 minutes. Serve very hot with a Madeira sauce (see basic recipe).

Pumpkin

1. Peel and cube the pumpkin.

Ingredients:
14 oz/400 g pumpkin
1 whole nutmeg
2 eggs
1 goat cheese
3½ tbsp/50 g butter
salt and pepper

Serves 4
Preparation time: 10 minutes
Cooking time: 25 minutes
Difficulty: ✳

2. Place the pumpkin in a pot, cover with cold water and lightly salt, then cover the pot and bring the water to a boil.

In French culinary terminology, *gratin* is synonymous with casserole, though in the world of casseroles, the *gratin* is king.

The secret of this recipe is the nutmeg, which brings out the subtle flavors of the nutrient-rich pumpkin. Like most squashes, pumpkin retains water. If you do not cook it until the day you prepare the gratin, it may prove close to impossible to dry it thoroughly. Our chef therefore suggests cooking the pumpkin a day in advance and letting it drain in a strainer until you are ready to use it. Do not add the pumpkin to boiling water, but add it to cold water and bring the water and pumpkin to a boil together in a covered pot. Once the water begins to boil, remove the cover and continue cooking for 25 minutes.

This is a very simple and inexpensive dish, a light accompaniment for all kinds of meat and poultry.

Try a red wine, perhaps a Sauvignon.

3. When the pumpkin is tender, drain the cubes thoroughly (overnight if desired). When ready to proceed, grind in a food mill or food processor.

4. Heat the pumpkin in a pan to allow excess moisture to evaporate. Add salt, pepper, and freshly-ground nutmeg to taste.

au Gratin

5. Beat the eggs and pour them into the pumpkin. Stir well. Remove from heat.

6. Pour the pumpkin into a baking dish. Sprinkle with the goat cheese and dot with the butter. Broil until the top is darkened and serve immediately.

Porcini

1. Slice the porcini and chop the shallot. Heat the walnut oil in a frying pan and brown the shallot in it.

Ingredients:
1 lb/500 g porcini
1 shallot
2 tbsp walnut oil
1 clove of garlic
sprigs of parsley
1 tsp chopped thyme
3 eggs
2/3 cup/150 ml crème
    fraîche
salt and pepper

Serves 5
Preparation time: 25 minutes
Cooking time: 35 minutes
Difficulty: ★★

2. Stir in the porcini until they spit back any moisture. Add salt and pepper. Chop the parsley and garlic.

Dariole is a French baker's term for both a certain cylindrical mold and the item baked in it, originally a pastry crust filled with a sweet cream. It is often cone-shaped and usually found in individual sizes. In Reims, darioles are encased in puff pastry for the feast of St. Remy.

Porcini mushrooms are in season twice a year. The first season is from May to June, sometimes even a little later. The very best time to enjoy them, however. is in the Fall. If fresh porcini are not available, dried are an acceptable alternative.

Our chef recommends placing aluminum foil on the baking sheet and adding water between it and the molds. The water will boil and create a bain marie, without allowing the the molds to move. This method prevents the creamy filling from seeping out and results in perfect *darioles*. This recipe calls for thyme, which is an unusual seasoning in combination with porcini mushrooms. The result, however, is pleasantly surprising.

Serve the *dariolles* alongside your choice of meat or game, perhaps with a red Bergerac.

3. Once the mushrooms have dried and all excess moisture has evaporated, stir in the parsley, garlic, and thyme. Combine thoroughly and remove from heat.

4. Chop the porcini by hand and place in a mixing bowl. Stir in the eggs. Add salt and pepper if necessary, and beat energetically until the eggs are well incorporated.

Darioles

5. Stir in the crème fraîche.

6. Pour the mixture into individual pre-buttered molds. Bake in a bain-marie at 325 °F for 20 minutes. Serve with the sauce used for the entrée.

Pumpkin and

1. Peel and cube the pumpkin. Place in a large pot.

Ingredients:
1 lb/500 g pumpkin
3 slices of French or
   Italian bread
2 cloves of garlic
6½ tbsp/100 ml milk
6½ tbsp/100 ml
   crème fraîche
scant ½ cup/100 g
   short-grain rice
2 large sprigs of
   parsley
2 eggs
¾ oz/20 g grated
   Swiss cheese
salt and pepper

Serves 6
Preparation time: 20 minutes
Cooking time: 50 minutes
Difficulty: ✲

2. Toast the bread and rub with the garlic. Add the bread to the pot and pour on the milk and crème fraîche. Sprinkle with salt and pepper. Let simmer until the pumpkin is tender but not overly soft.

In Provence, a *tian* is a ceramic casserole dish that has been used so commonly for making gratins that the words *gratin* and *tian* have become interchangeable. This recipe, however, hearkens back to the idea of a baked casserole, which might originally have been baked in an earthenware *tian*.

In the south of France, a kind of whole-grain local rice was usually chosen for this recipe because of its rich, wheaty texture; unfortunately, though, its nutritional value was the same as that of white rice. Our chef recommends a round rice from Camargue.

The pumpkin needs to be puréed thoroughly but should remain very thick. You may try substituting zucchini for pumpkin, but if you do, you will need to use two additional eggs. It is also possible to prepare the purée the night before.

The mold should be buttered and floured, or use a nonstick mold. Individual molds require less baking time. The *tian* should cool for about 15 minutes before it is removed from the mold.

This dish should be served warm as an accompaniment for pork or veal. It can also be served cold in the summer with a vegetable sauce. It may be refrigerated up to four or five days and reheated in a bain-marie. Add a sprinkling of fresh ground pepper just before serving.

Try serving this tian with a red Bandol, of the Provence region, of course.

3. Blend with an electric beater or food processor to produce a thick purée.

4. Chop the parsley. Stir the pre-cooked rice and parsley into the purée.

Rice Tian

5. Add the eggs and cheese. Stir all ingredients until thoroughly blended.

6. Spoon the mixture into a buttered mold. Bake in a bain-marie at 350 °F for about 40 minutes. Serve with a tomato sauce, if desired.

Artichoke and

1. Combine the yeast and 1 cup/250 ml lukewarm milk. Stir in 3½ tbsp/25 g flour; let rest. Separately, mix the remaining milk and flour, 2 eggs yolks and a little salt. Whip the egg whites and fold in; blend in the crème fraîche. Let rest. Combine the mixtures and chill.

2. Boil the artichokes in salted water. Scrape the flesh off each leaf and combine with the anchovy fillets, chopped garlic, parsley and chervil, and 2 1/2 tbsp/40 g of butter. Set aside.

Ingredients:
⅓ oz/10 g yeast
1⅔ cup/400 ml lukewarm milk
1¼ cups/150 g flour
2 eggs, separated
3½ tbsp/50 ml crème fraîche
4 artichokes
4 anchovy fillets, in oil
1 clove of garlic; 2 sprigs of parsley; 1 bunch of chervil
6½ tbsp/100 g butter
12 bay scallops
2 shallots
1 tbsp red peppercorns
6½ tbsp/100 ml white wine
juice of a lemon wedge
salt and pepper

Serves 4
Preparation time: 1 hour 10 minutes
Cooking time: 40 minutes
Resting time: 2 hours
Difficulty: ✶✶

The blini comes to us from Eastern Europe and adds a Russian touch to this uncommon medley of flavors. Usually served with caviar or smoked salmon, they are traditionally made in a special small frying pan, about 4-5 inches (10-12 cm) in diameter, that gives them their characteristic perfectly round form. Though it is a handy kitchen utensil that you may find useful in general, a blini pan is not a must. Blini can also be shaped by placing a round cookie cutter or an empty tuna can with both sides removed inside a larger non-stick frying pan.

Our chef recommends letting the blini batter sit for two hours so that the yeast has time to rise. This will prevent the blini from becoming too thick as they cook, and will make the resulting pancakes much lighter. The order in which ingredients are added is very important, so be sure to follow the directions exactly.

The best way to remove the prickly choke of the artichoke is to break off the stem on the bottom. Cutting off the stem only makes the process more difficult.

A good white Sancerre is the perfect wine to bring out the original flavors of this dish.

3. Heat some oil in a frying pan (or blini pan). Place a cookie cutter or other round form in it and make the blini.

4. Cut the scallops in half. Lightly salt and pepper them, then sear them in a hot pan. Set aside.

Scallop Blinis

5. Finely chop the shallots and stir them into the pan used to sear the scallops. Add the peppercorns, then deglaze with the wine. Let the sauce reduce, then whisk in the remaining butter and a few drops of lemon juice.

6. Spread the artichoke butter on the blini. Arrange the scallops in a circle on a serving dish. Pour the pepper-butter sauce over the scallops and serve.

Porcini-Stuffed

1. Bring a pot of lightly salted water to a boil. Blanch the whole cabbage leaves and immediately douse in cold water to halt cooking. Set aside.

Ingredients:
1 large cabbage
8 porcini mushrooms
2 tbsp/10 ml olive oil
2 slices of prosciutto
4 shallots
1 onion
1 clove of garlic
1 bunch of parsley
2 branches of chervil
1 bunch of chives
1 cube chicken
  bouillon
⅔ cup/150 ml crème
  fraîche
salt and pepper

Serves 4
Preparation time: 45 minutes
Cooking time: 35 minutes
Difficulty: ✷✷

2. Peel and dice the porcini. Cook them in a little olive oil over high heat.

In the Fall the beautiful region of Sens harbors one of France's great culinary treasures: porcini mushrooms. Along with enjoying the autumn foliage, picking mushrooms is a seasonal pleasure.

Be sure to remove the hard, indigestible, unappetizing outer leaves of the cabbage, and baste the stuffed cabbages often as they bake so that they do not dry out. Alternatively, they could also be steamed.

It is especially important to add the garlic and herbs toward the end of the preparation so that they retain as much of their distinct flavors as possible. The stuffing can be made with different meats. This recipe calls for prosciutto, but cured beef, leftover meat or poultry would also be interesting variations.

Stuffed cabbage is a heartwarming, rustic dish, and has been ennobled in this recipe by the addition of flavorful porcini mushrooms.

Our wine expert recommends a red wine, perhaps a Julienas.

3. Chop the prosciutto and add it to the mushrooms. Peel and chop the shallots and onion, and stir into the mushrooms as well. Slowly sauté these ingredients over low heat.

4. Salt and pepper lightly. Chop the garlic and herbs and introduce them into the mixture. Separately, dissolve the bouillon cube in 1/2 cup of boiling water. Set aside.

Cabbage

5. Stir ⅓ of crème fraîche into the mushroom mixture and reduce for a few minutes.

6. Lay the blanched cabbage leaves on sheets of plastic wrap. Top each with stuffing, close the leaves and enclose in plastic wrap. Place in a baking dish with the bouillon. Bake 20 minutes at 300 °F. Remove from oven, strain the bouillon, and reduce over low heat. Add the remaining crème fraîche, reduce briefly and serve.

Oysters and

1. Clean the spinach and blanch it for a few seconds. Hold it under cold water to stop the cooking process, then set aside. Open the oysters. Remove them from their shell and place in a strainer.

Ingredients:
1 lb/500 g spinach
24 oysters
6½ tbsp/100 ml fish stock (see basic recipe)
1 shallot
3½ tbsp/50 g butter
6½ tbsp/100 ml crème fraîche
juice of 1 lemon
1 egg yolk
1 cucumber
salt and pepper

Serves 4
Preparation time: 15 minutes
Cooking time: 20 minutes
Difficulty: ✶✶

2. Poach the oysters in the fish stock.

Traditionally, the "r" months, from September to April, are the months of the sea; these are the months in which to enjoy oysters. At any time, you can ascertain the freshness of oysters by holding them upside down: if water leaks out, the oysters are not fresh enough. If oysters are unavailable, mussels could also be used in this recipe. Leeks can also be substituted for the spinach for a somewhat different twist.

The success of this recipe depends primarily on cooking the oysters precisely the right length of time. They should be blanched for no more than 30 seconds, or they will become chewy and tasteless.

For an attractive presentation, display the oysters on a bed of rock salt; this will keep them from wobbling and brings a hint of the ocean to your table.

These oysters should be served warm and eaten immediately.

A secret offered up by our wine expert is an ancient affinity between the sea and Muscadet, perhaps a Muscadet sur lie.

3. Chop the shallots and brown them in a little butter, then mix in the spinach. Salt and pepper lightly.

4. Reduce the liquid used to poach the oysters to ¾ its original volume. Stir in 1 tbsp of crème fraîche and the lemon juice.

Cucumbers au Gratin

5. Whip the rest of the crème fraîche until it resembles whipped cream, then whisk in the egg yolk. Fold into the oyster sauce. Adjust seasoning if necessary.

6. Dab a little spinach in each oyster shell, then place an oyster on each bed of spinach. Fill the shells with sauce. Broil just for a minute or two. Peel and julienne the cucumber. Blanch for a few seconds and sprinkle over the broiled oysters.

Veal Sweetbreads

Ingredients:
2.2 lbs/1 kg veal
    sweetbreads
6½ tbsp/100 ml
    vinegar
1 glass of white wine
3 large onions
6½ tbsp/100 g butter
1 tsp sugar
6½ tbsp/100 ml oil
1 cube of veal
    bouillon
⅔ cup/150 ml crème
    fraîche
salt and pepper

Serves 6
Preparation time: 20 minutes
Cooking time: 50 minutes
Difficulty: ✶

1. Blanch the sweetbreads in a pot of boiling water with half the vinegar. Remove from the boiling water and plunge into cold water. Then poach the meat in water with half a glass of white wine. Add salt and pepper.

The onion is the oldest vegetable known in human cuisine, and it is the foundation of all French cooking. Egyptians idolized the onion and considered it as important as any god. The physician Ambroise Pare thought it the antidote to many poisons. The onion family is vast, incorporating not only the many different varieties of onions but also its many relatives, such as the leek. Whether purple or white, small or large, the presence of onion in soup or sauce is unmistakeable and often indepensible, as well.

Sweetbreads are an animal's thalamus gland. They are easy to digest and high in protein. Our chef suggests soaking the sweetbreads in cold water for at least one hour, and as long as overnight, before blanching them for about ten minutes in unsalted water.

The chef suggests a celery purée or some variation of cabbage as an accompaniment. to this succulent dish. Serve these sweetbreads hot.

After smelling this dish being prepared, no guest will be able to resist it.

2. Slice the sweetbreads and set aside. Peel and slice the onions.

3. Carefully brown the onions in a large pot with 2 tbsp of butter. Add the sugar and the remaining vinegar. Let the onions caramelize.

4. Sauté the sweetbread slices in a separate pan with the rest of the butter and the oil. Turn often. Set aside to cool.

with Caramelized Onions

5. Deglaze the pan and add the onions. Stir in the remaining white wine and reduce.

6. Dissolve the bouillon in 6½ tbsp/100 ml water and add to the pan. Stir in the crème fraîche. Simmer until the mixture thickens. To serve, place the onions on a serving platter and crown with the sweetbreads. Serve very warm.

Ardennes

1. Peel the artichokes, cut off the stems, and rub with a lemon half. Mix the flour with a little water and the juice of half a lemon. Pour the flour mixture into a pot of lightly salted water with the artichokes and bring to a boil.

2. Peel and chop the shallots. Dice the ham finely.

Ingredients:
4 artichokes
1 lemon
6½ tbsp/50 g flour
3 shallots
4 slices Ardennes ham
7 oz/200 g mushrooms
2 cups/500 ml
   langoustine consommé
   (see basic recipe)
6½ tbsp/100 ml crème
   fraîche
3½ tbsp/50 g butter
14 oz/400 g pike mousse
   (see basic recipe)
12 langoustines
1 bouquet garni
salt and pepper

Serves 4
Preparation time: 30 minutes
Cooking time: 55 minutes
Difficulty: ★★

Ham from the Ardennes in northeastern France is famous. This particular dish won first prize in 1986 at Brillat-Savarin for the best recipe with Ardennes ham. Our chef suggests unsmoked ham, blanched to reduce the saltiness and patted dry to minimize moisture. The langoustines are an interesting touch, but shrimp or crayfish could also be substituted.

Cook the artichokes only briefly in boiling water in Step One, since they will be cooked again in the oven. The sauce in which they are blanched will help them retain their color during cooking.

All the ingredients for the stuffing should be cold when combined.

This dish is best served warm, but because it is prepared in two stages, it can be prepared in the evening and baked the following day.

A dry white wine, such as a Bourgogne, should serve to harmonize the many different flavors incorporated in this dish.

3. Chop the mushrooms in a food processor. For the sauce, reduce the langoustine consommé to half its original volume, then add the crème fraîche. Reduce further, then set aside.

4. Lightly brown the chopped shallots in a large pot with 1 tbsp of butter, then add the mushrooms. Let this mixture cook until it is completely dry. Add salt and pepper.

Ham Surprises

5. Once the artichokes are done, let them cool in the cooking liquid. Remove the prickly choke. Prepare the pike mousse according to the basic recipe for fish mousse. Stir the ham and mushrooms into the mousse to make the filling. Mix well.

6. Stuff the artichokes, top with a dollop of butter, and bake at 300 °F for 20 minutes. Poach the langoustines with the bouquet garni. To serve, decorate each articoke with 3 langoustine tails and surround with sauce. Serve warm.

Sorrel

1. Remove all bones from the fish and brown in the butter and oil. Add salt, pepper, and the MacCormick seasoning. Remove from the pan and cool. Blanch the spinach briefly.

2. Chop the shallots, sorrel and parsley. In the same pan used for the fish, brown the shallots, then add the blanched spinach and sorrel. Sprinkle with MacCormick seasoning.

3. Stir in the parsley and the white wine. Reduce this mixture and divide it in half. Prepare the fish mousse according to the basic recipe.

Ingredients:
For the pâté:
1 lb/500 g monkfish
3 tbsp/45 g butter
2 tbsp/30 ml oil
1¾ oz/50 g spinach
2 shallots
fresh sorrel and parsley
⅔ cup/150 ml white wine
14 oz/400 g fish mousse
3½ oz/100 g choux pastry, salted
MacCormick Seafood Seasoning; salt and pepper
For the sauce:
2 tbsp/30 ml white wine
4 tsp/20 ml crème fraîche
4 egg yolks
butter
salt and pepper

Serves 6
Preparation time: 45 minutes
Cooking time: 1 hour 15 minutes
Difficulty: ✳✳

Here is a wonderful fish appetizer. The natural acidity of the sorrel—which is at the same time low in calories and high in potassium, magnesium, and vitamin C—will highlight the nuances of all the other flavors.

Although this recipe calls for monkfish, it can also be prepared with lobster, salmon, or a variety of other fishes. Our chef warns that the fish used must be very cold, almost frozen, in order to create a mousse with the proper texture. To prevent the monkfish from contorting in odd shapes during cooking, be sure to remove the nerves completely.

For a truly elegant play on color, this recipe can become a tri-color mousse. To do so, divide the mousse into three parts. Leave one third a pure fish mousse, another third takes on the green of the sorrel and spinach, and the remaining portion can be tinted pink with a touch of tomato paste. Your guests cannot fail to be impressed.

This pâté can be prepared some time in advance and kept in a warm oven.

Our wine expert recommends a Pouilly-Fuissé. Alert and bold, this great wine will add to the general success of the meal.

4. For the sauce, add the additional white wine to one half of the spinach and herb mixture. Bring to a boil and reduce briefly, then whisk in the crème fraîche and egg yolks. Set aside. In a separate bowl, energetically stir the choux pastry into the fish mousse.

Monkfish Pâté

5. Stir ¼ of the fish mousse mixture into the remaining spinach and herbs. Blend well. Butter a loaf pan. Spread a generous layer of white fish mousse in the bottom of the pan, then add a layer of herbed fish mousse.

6. Place the monkfish on top of the green mousse. Cover it with the remaining herbed mousse, then with the white mousse. Bake in a bain-marie for 1 hour at 350 °F. Gently simmer the sauce, then whisk in a blender. Adjust the seasoning, if necessary, and whip in some butter. Serve the sauce and the pâté together.

Kidney and

1. Blanch the sweetbreads in boiling water for 5 minutes. Boil a separate pot of water with a little salt and pepper. Add the onion, 1 carrot, the bouquet garni and the wine. Add the blanched sweetbreads and simmer for 15 minutes.

2. Peel the small onions and 2 remaining carrots. Poach them separately in slightly salted boiling water. Slice the mushrooms and lightly sauté them. Set these vegetables aside.

Ingredients:
1 lb/500 g veal
  sweetbreads
1 onion
3 carrots
1 bouquet garni
¾ cup/200 ml white wine
1 handful small white
  onions
4 mushrooms
2 veal kidneys
6½ tbsp/100 g butter
3½ tbsp/50 ml Calvados
  brandy
¾ cup/200 ml crème
  fraîche
¾ cup plus 1 tbsp/100 g
  flour
salt and pepper

Serves 4
Preparation time: 15 minutes
Cooking time: 40 minutes
Difficulty: ★★

Traditionally, this type of stew is prepared with white meats and organ meats and served with a white sauce, which led to its original French name, *Blanquette*. However, this simple and quick recipe can also be made with basil and tomatoes instead of the onions, mushrooms, and carrots used in our chef's version here.

Our chef suggests cutting the kidneys in order to remove the fat most effectively. In addition, the sweetbreads should be soaked in cold water for several hours before cooking. It is also important that they not be overcooked.

Try serving this savory stew with green beans or zuccini. It should be served warm but can be reheated up to a day later. It is a perfect meal to serve among friends.

Since white wines enliven any white organ meat, our wine expert has chosen a Chablis Montée-de-Tonnerre.

3. Remove the fat from the kidneys, taking particular care to also remove the central nerve. Cut the kidneys into cubes and flour them. Sauté in a frying pan in the butter.

4. Once the sweetbreads are firm, cut them up and add to the kidneys. Sauté together for several minutes. Add salt and pepper.

Sweetbread Stew

5. Deglaze the pan by pouring the brandy over the meats, and flambé.

6. Stir in the mushrooms. Pour in the crème fraîche and simmer for about 10 minutes. Adjust seasoning if necessary. Add the onions and carrots from Step 2. Serve warm with rice, potatoes, or french fries.

Liver in

1. Salt and pepper the liver, then coat the slices in flour.

Ingredients:
4 slices veal liver
¼ cup flour
6½ tbsp/100 g butter
2 shallots
⅔ cup/150 ml
  raspberry vinegar
3½ oz/100 g
  raspberries
6½ tbsp/100 ml heavy
  cream
salt and pepper

Serves 4
Preparation time: 10 minutes
Cooking time: 20 minutes
Difficulty: ✶

2. In a pan with 2 tbsp of butter, fry the liver to your taste.

Of all the varieties of liver, veal liver is our chef's favorite. It has a pale pink tone while the others are red; it is firm yet it will melt in your mouth, and it is extremely rich in vitamin D, calcium's precious ally.

Some say that liver should never be cooked to the point where the inside is any darker than the original pink. Others prefer to cook it through. Since the best school of thought on the matter is one's own, cook it to your liking.

Raspberry vinegar is a traditional vinegar that has been made for centuries. Louis Pasteur explained the process of fermentation that transforms wine to acid in the 19th century, though vinegar has been used since the days of the Roman Empire and was even diluted with water and drunk as a beverage.

To accentuate the beauty of this dish, add a few fresh raspberries to the sauce just before serving, as well as a few leaves of basil or tarragon.

The flavor of raspberry is quite fine and striking and should be accompanied by something that will not overpower it, such as French fries or potato chips.

Our wine expert suggests a Gros Plant from Nantes.

3. Peel and chop the shallots.

4. In the same frying pan used for the liver, add 1 more tbsp of butter and brown the shallots.

Raspberry Vinaigrette

5. Pour in the vinegar and reduce a few minutes.

6. Add the raspberries and heat briefly, then pour in the crème fraîche. Add salt and pepper. Mix with a blender and pour the sauce through a strainer to remove seeds. Whisk in the remaining butter over low heat. Serve the liver slices with the sauce.

Sweetbreads

1. Peel the asparagus, then poach in boiling water. Do not overcook; they should be crisp. Cut off the tips and set aside. Purée the rest.

Ingredients:
2.2 lbs/1 kg asparagus
2.2 lbs/1 kg
   sweetbreads
1 cup/120 g flour
3½ tbsp/50 g butter
3½ tbsp/50 ml
   Calvados brandy
6½ tbsp/100 ml crème
   fraîche
1 cup white wine
1 bouquet garni
1 onion
2 carrots
whole peppercorns
salt and pepper

Serves 6
Preparation time: 10 minutes
Cooking time: 30 minutes
Difficulty: ✶

2. After soaking the sweetbreads in cold water for at least 2 hours, blanch them in lightly salted water.

While our chef has a special fondness for sweetbreads, in this recipe they could also be replaced by duck or even veal cutlets. Let the sweetbreads soak in cold water overnight so that they become white.

Because asparagus have such strong fibers, they need to be cut into smaller pieces before blending them in a food processor.

This dish must be served very hot. It can be reheated and can be stored up to three days in the refrigerator. It is an ideal treat for a special family gathering.

The tenderness of organ meats should be reinforced by a fairly aggressive wine, such as a white Mercurey.

3. Cut the poached sweetbreads into medium-sized pieces. Coat with flour. Melt the butter and sauté the meat. Add salt and pepper.

4. Once the sweetbreads have taken on a little color, pour the Calvados over them and flambé.

with Asparagus

5. Add the crème fraîche and simmer for 10 to 15 minutes.

6. Remove the sweetbreads. Add the asparagus purée and bring to a boil, stirring often. Cover the sweetbreads in this sauce. Serve warm with the asparagus tips.

Salmon

Ingredients:

1 lb/500 g tomatoes
¾ cup/200 ml olive oil
7 oz/200 g onions, chopped
1 bouquet garni
1 red pepper
1 green pepper
8¾ oz/250 g zucchini
1 tbsp tomato paste
8 slices of salmon
10 black olives

Serves 6
Preparation time: 40 minutes
Cooking time: 30 minutes
Difficulty: ✳✳

1. Brown the onions; set aside. Peel, seed and dice ⅔ of the tomatoes. Sauté in a little olive oil, lightly salt and pepper, add the bouquet garni, then set aside with half the onions. Peel, seed, dice and lightly sauté the peppers with the remaining onions.

Salmon is both a freshwater and a saltwater fish, though the salmon found in French stores these days most likely come from the waters of the North Pacific or North Atlantic. The beauty of this recipe is its marriage of tastes from North and South: Salmon generally live in deep, cold waters, but the other ingredients used here come from warmer climes.

The preparation requires some patience, for the vegetables should be cut into small pieces. Keep in mind, however, that the smaller the vegetables are diced, the less time it will take to cook them, so be careful not to overcook. To know when to add the tomatoes to the other vegetables, keep your eyes on the color of the zucchini: When their green color begins to fade, stir in the tomatoes.

The *galette*, originally a round, flat cake, is in this instance made without a traditional crust. Thin salmon fillets form a kind of shell for the filling. Use a spatula and plastic wrap to gently place the Salmon *Galette* in the steamer without breaking it.

You might try substituting bass or pike in this recipe. Just be sure to use a fish that does not crumble easily. Moreover, the *galette* may be prepared in advance and steamed just before serving. Serve warm. The Loire valley's most famous wine will be able to defend its reputation during this meal; we recommend a white Sancerre.

2. Dice the zucchini. When the peppers are nearly cooked, add the zucchini. Lightly salt and pepper.

3. Peel, seed, and dice the remaining tomatoes and add to the mini-ratatouille. Finish cooking over low heat. Stir the tomato paste into the tomatoes from Step 1.

4. To form the galette, line the ring of a springform pan with plastic wrap and place 4 slices of salmon inside. Let the salmon cover the edge of the pie ring. Once the ratatouille has cooled, fill the salmon-lined ring with it.

Galette

5. Cover the ratatouille with the remaining salmon slices. Lightly salt and pepper, then enfold in plastic wrap.

6. Steam the galette for 15 minutes. Whip the tomato and tomato paste mixture with olive oil. Adjust seasonings to taste. Serve the galette garnished with the olives and the whipped tomato sauce.

Brussel Sprouts

Ingredients:
1 lb/500 g brussel
 sprouts
1 cup/250 ml crème
 fraîche
3½ oz/100 g onions
6½ tbsp/100 ml white
 wine
1⅔ lbs/800 g mussels
3½ tbsp/50 g butter
chives
salt and pepper

Serves 4
Preparation time: 20 minutes
Cooking time: 40 minutes
Difficulty: *

1. Blanch the brussel sprouts in slightly salted boiling water, then strain and rinse under cold running water to stop the cooking process. Only then, boil them in salted water. When tender, purée with a food mill or food processor.

This recipe is an original combination of the distinctive flavor of brussel sprouts and the softer taste of the mussels. The two together, by the way, offer considerable nutrition: This dish is rich in potassium, sulfur, and several vitamins. Our chef suggests using the cultivated mussels from Bouchot, which are particularly flavorful, but other mussels will certainly do.

To remove the acidity from the onions and the wine, let that mixture boil for several minutes. Do not forget to blanch the sprouts well to revitalize them and take the edge off their often strong taste.

Purées and mousses always add a welcome lightness and elegance to a meal. During mussel season, you and your guests will surely appreciate this one.

Eastern France produces many good wines that are often overlooked. Our wine expert suggests righting this wrong by serving a white Mercurey.

2. In a saucepan, bring ⅔ of the crème fraîche to a boil. Salt and pepper lightly.

3. Stir in the brussel sprout purée and mix vigorously. Let this mixture thicken.

4. Chop the onions and sauté them with the wine. Let simmer. Add the mussels and let them open. Once cooled, remove the mussels from their shell.

and Mussels

5. Pour the liquid used to steam the mussels through a strainer and reduce it to ¾ its initial volume. Stir in the remaining crème fraîche and reduce. Once the sauce is smooth, enrich with the butter.

6. Stir the mussels into the sauce just before serving. Adjust seasoning if necessary. Place the brussel sprout purée in the center of a serving dish and surround it with the mussels in their sauce. Sprinkle with a few chives.

Chestnut-Stuffed

1. With a paring knife, peel the chestnuts. Blanch them in a pot of slightly salted boiling water. While still warm, peel off the thin inner skins.

Ingredients:
1 lb/500 g chestnuts
4 cups/1 l water
1 cube of beef
   bouillon
1 stalk of celery
1 cabbage
3½ tbsp/50 g butter
salt and pepper

Serves 6
Preparation time: 35 minutes
Cooking time: 45 minutes
Difficulty: ✶✶

This vegetarian dish is one of a kind. The combination of chestnuts and cabbage is delightful, and does full justice to the flavor of the chestnut, which is not often prepared in such a savory manner. Chestnuts have basically the same nutrients as wheat, and are high in calories.

When stuffing the cabbage leaf-lined ramekins, pack the stuffing as densely as possible and try to avoid leaving any pockets of air. This will make it much easier to unmold them and help them maintain their shape on the plate.

This appetizer is a lovely an accompaniment for game.

The Rhône valley, we are told, produces spicy wines that are at home on fall and winter tables. Our wine expert suggests serving a red Crozes-Hermitage.

2. Dissolve the bouillon cube in 4 cups/1 liter boiling water and whisk well. Add the celery and boil the chestnuts in this liquid.

3. In a slightly salted pot of water to boil, blanch the cabbage leaves. Discard the tough, indigestible outer edges.

4. Butter ramekins or other individual molds and line each one with a cabbage leaf.

Cabbage

5. Once the chestnuts are cooked thoroughly, mash them with a fork and reduce the resulting purée until it thickens. Fill the molds with the chestnuts and fold the cabbage leaf over the purée.

6. Steam the stuffed cabbage leaves for 20 minutes. Serve with game, poultry, or a roast.

Salmon and

1. Fillet the salmon (see basic recipe). Brown the bone, cover with water, add the chopped carrot and onion, and let simmer. Peel and finely chop the shallots, then brown them. Slice all the mushrooms and add to the shallots. Salt and pepper and let simmer.

2. Let the moisture from the mushrooms evaporate. Stir in the crème fraîche and gently combine. Chop the parsley and stir it in, then let the mixture cool.

Ingredients:
1⅓ lbs/600 g salmon
1 carrot
1 onion
2 shallots
5¼ oz/150 g chanterelles
5¼ oz/150 g white mushrooms
5¼ oz/150 g porcini
5¼ oz/150 g trompette de la mort mushrooms
⅔ cup/150 ml crème fraîche
3 sprigs of parsley
8 ¾ oz/250 g spinach
13 tbsp/200 g butter
1 tbsp/15 g salmon eggs
boiling onions to garnish
salt and pepper

Serves 6
Preparation time: 35 minutes
Cooking time: 30 minutes
Difficulty: ★★

A true connoisseur knows *millefeuille*, a puff pastry concoction that is a specialty of French cuisine. Here, it does away with sugar and becomes a beautiful pie filled with salmon and a medley of different mushrooms.

The salmon should be thinly sliced. If necessary, use a meat tenderizer to pound it thin, though you should protect it with two sheets of paper. To prevent the salmon from becoming dry during cooking, steam it slowly and do not overcook! This recipe can also be prepared with bass.

Just about any variety of mushroom can be incorporated into this recipe; play with the flavors and follow your own taste. The butter must be very hard and cold when added to the sauce so that it will melt slowly and thicken the sauce optimally. Add a few drops of lemon juice at the end of the preparation.

Once the *millefeuille* is on the serving dish, remove the wax paper and flan ring, and flank the *millefeuille* with spinach leaves. Our chef has chosen to decorate with small boiling onions, but one could also make an attractive presentation with zucchini.

The *millefeuille* can be prepared the night before and steamed at the last minute. Serve it warm. You may serve it lukewarm, but it cannot be reheated.

Salmon loves a Sauvignon. So serve one of the best to help preserve the lightness of the *millefeuille*, a Pouilly-Fumé (Baron de L.).

3. Place a sheet of buttered wax paper on a cookie sheet. Set a flan ring or circle from a springform pan on it. Slice the salmon and line the ring with several slices. Add salt and pepper. Cover with a layer of the mushroom mixture.

4. Add another layer of salmon slices, then more mushrooms. Salt and pepper lightly. Cover with the remaining salmon.

Mushroom Millefeuille

5. Lightly blanch the spinach in slightly salted water. Run the spinach under cold water to halt the cooking, then strain. Remove the fish bones from their liquid. Whisk in the butter, adjust the seasoning, and set aside.

6. Steam the galette. Before serving, remove the metal ring and wax paper, and surround the millefeuille with spinach leaves. Cover with sauce. Decorate with salmon eggs and boiling onions, and serve warm.

Sweetbreads

1. Soak the sweetbreads in cold water overnight. Blanch them in water with the vinegar, then douse in cold water. Sear them in a frying pan with the oil. Add salt and pepper. Cube the onion and carrot and brown them with the sweetbreads.

2. Once these have browned well, dissolve the bouillon cube in ¾ cup/200 ml water, and use this to deglaze the frying pan. Add the bouquet garni. Cover and simmer for 20 minutes. Salt and pepper to taste.

3. Lightly blanch the spinach in a pot of salted water, then sauté in a pan with a little butter. Sprinkle with salt and pepper. Slice the mushrooms and sauté separately. Chop the shallots and add to the mushrooms.

Ingredients:
1⅓ lbs/600 g veal
   sweetbreads
6½ tbsp/100 ml vinegar
2 tbsp/30 ml oil
1 onion
1 carrot
1 beef bouillon cube
1 bouquet garni
8¾ oz/250 g spinach
3½ oz/100 g mushrooms
2 shallots
¾ cup/200 ml crème
   fraîche
10 tbsp/150 g butter
1 bunch of chervil
salt and freshly ground
   pepper

Serves 4
Preparation time: 35 minutes
Cooking time: 35 minutes
Difficulty: ✶✶

Sweetbreads are one of our chef's favorite organ meats. To blanch them, cover them with cold water and bring the water to a boil with the sweetbreads in it. Then press the sweetbreads for two hours by wrapping them in a dish towel and setting them between two cutting boards to squeeze out excess water.

After blanching the spinach, strain it well, even squeezing it gently between your hands. While ordinary mushrooms will do nicely in this recipe, chanterelles or porcini would add an extra flavor accent. And you could use sorrel instead of spinach; it will add tang but is less attractive when cooked.

If the sauce becomes too thick, dilute it with a little water. This dish can be prepared in advance, but no more than a day.

Our wine expert recommends serving these sweetbreads with a great white wine, such as a Puligny-Montrachet (Les Flatières).

4. Once the sweetbreads are done, add the crème fraîche, stirring gently. Remove the sweetbreads and continue to simmer for about 5 minutes.

à la Veronique

5. Pour the sauce through a strainer, then enrich it by whipping in the butter. Set aside. Thinly slice the sweetbreads and line individual-size baking dishes with them.

6. Add a layer of spinach, then mushrooms, and repeat the process until the dishes are full. Press down on the ingredients so that the filling is compact. Turn over onto a serving dish and coat with the sauce. Garnish with chervil and serve warm.

Potato

1. Peel the potatoes.

Ingredients:
8 potatoes
4 cups/1 l oil
salt and pepper

Serves 4
Preparation time: 20 minutes
Cooking time: 20 minutes
Difficulty: ✷✷

2. Trim the potatoes to accentuate their round shape.

Finally we learn the secret to potato puffs! Our chef reports, amusingly, that this potato dish was the product of pure serendipity: King Louis-Philippe was overseeing the construction of a railway. A chef had been awaiting the king's arrival and had prepared a meal. The train was late, of course, and the meal was cold by the time the king arrived. So the cook put the potato chips in to fry again and found that they swelled up. This is a perfect example of fate waving its wand over culinary history.

The oil in which the potatoes are fried should be heated to its smoke point; it will cool when the potatoes are immersed. Use a pot with high edges so that you can hold and shake it. This aggitation allows air to enter the oil and makes the chips swell. The potato slices can all be cooked at once as long as they do not stick to each other.

Between the first and second dunking, the chips should sit on paper towels to drain excess grease. They should be fried the second time immediately before serving.

This recipe is not difficult, but it does takes practice. These potatoes are a perfect accompaniment for a meat dish or a BBQ. But on your first attempt, be sure to invite friends who are easy to please. Now, well armed with these instructions, the adventure begins...

The choice of wine depends on the meat being served, but a Savigny-lès-Beaune or a Pomerol would be nice.

3. Cut the potatoes into ¼ in/5 mm-thick slices.

4. Heat the oil to its smoking point in a large pot with high sides and handles. Drop the potato slices into the oil and stir.

Puffs

5. As the slices are frying, shake the pot from time to time so that the slices are well-coated in oil and bump into each other.

6. Heat a second pot of oil. Just before serving, drop the potato slices into this pot and fry again. Drain and serve.

Stuffed Peppers

1. For the stuffing, peel and chop the shallots, garlic, and onions, and brown lightly in a little butter. Seed and dice the tomatoes, add to the onion, and sauté until the tomatoes are tender. Set aside.

2. Hollow out the peppers. Grind the beef, veal and ham in a meat grinder. Quarter the tomatoes for the coulis; peel and chop the onions, carrots, and shallots. Set aside.

3. Mix the beef, veal and ham together very thoroughly. Add the eggs. Combine with the sautéed tomatoes and onions. Stir well.

Ingredients:
1¾ oz/50 g shallots
1 clove of garlic
2¾ oz/80 g onions
5 oz/140 g tomatoes
4 green peppers
6 oz/170 g beef
12 oz/340 g veal *and* ham
3 eggs
4 tbsp/60 ml olive oil
For the coulis:
4½ lbs/2 kg tomatoes
3½ tbsp/50 g butter
1 oz/30 g onions
4 oz/110 g carrots
2 oz/70 g shallots
3 cloves of garlic
1 bouquet garni
2 tsp sugar
salt and pepper

Serves 6
Preparation time: 40 minutes
Cooking time: 40 minutes
Difficulty: ✳

This is another classic recipe that our chef has rediscovered and slightly updated. Following an honored tradition, our chef has found a new flavor by re-creating the old. This is the perfect dish to shake things up a little.

One important tip: Be sure to cover the peppers in foil while baking to keep their skins from burning. Where once upon a time, our grandparents' generation may have had the time to keep a loving eye on the oven, today's cook has much less time to spend tied to the stove.

These peppers can be accompanied by a creole rice. They can also be served cold. The flavors of the stuffing seem only to improve over time, and should there be any leftover peppers, they will taste exquisite.

The elegant and sharp side of a Bandol Blanc de Blanc will complement the exuberance of the peppers.

4. Coat the bottom of a baking pan with the olive oil. Fill the peppers with the stuffing. Place in the dish and bake for at least 1 hour at 300 °F.

with Tomato Coulis

5. For the coulis, sauté the chopped onions, carrots, shallots and garlic in a pot with butter. Add the quartered tomatoes, bouquet garni, and sugar. Add water to cover the vegetables. Let simmer for approximately 20 minutes. Add salt and pepper as needed.

6. Remove the bouquet garni. Purée the coulis with a blender and pour through a strainer. Adjust seasoning. Pour the coulis on a serving platter. Slice the peppers and arrange them on the plate.

Foie Gras and

1. Remove the langoustines from their shell. Salt them, then brown them over high heat with some of the butter. Set aside.

Ingredients:
2.2 lbs/1 kg
  langoustines
3½ tbsp/50 g butter
2 dozen radishes
6½ tbsp/100 ml wine
  vinegar
7 oz/200 g fresh foie
  gras
1 cube of veal
  bouillon
2 cups/500 ml water
1 shallot
4 small brioches
salt and pepper

Serves 4
Preparation time: 20 minutes
Cooking time: 35 minutes
Difficulty: ✶✶

2. Clean the radishes. Pour the vinegar into a pot of boiling salted water and blanch the radishes in this mixture.

This recipe successfully combines the elegance of langoustines with the aristocratic foie gras in individual brioches. To save a considerable amount of time, you may buy brioches instead of making them from scratch. However, if you happen to have some leftover brioche pastry, this would be an excellent use for it.

Do not sauté the shallot until the langoustines are almost done. This will keep it from burning. Because the foie gras has a high fat content, no additional butter or oil is necessary to sauté it. Also, remember that foie gras dissolves very quickly, so sear it well and keep an eye on it.

The sauce can be served on the side. The foie gras must be eaten warm, whether the sauce is ready or not!

Try a Savennières, Clos-du-Papillon. This great white wine from Anjou blends its delicate aromas with the scent of vegetables. It is still almost unknown, so open a bottle and enjoy.

3. Slice the foie gras and set aside. Dissolve the bouillon cube in ½ cup water.

4. Peel and chop the shallot and add it to the langoustines. Brown them well. Once browned, pour off the excess grease and pour the veal stock over the langoustines. Deglaze the pan and set aside.

Langoustine Brioche

5. In a nonstick frying pan, sear the foie gras slices. Lightly salt and pepper and set aside.

6. Slice off the top of each brioche and hollow out the inside. Just before serving, combine the langoustines and the foie gras in the pan and bring to a slight boil. Fill the brioche with the meats and serve warm with the radishes and sauce.

Ingredients:
16 chicken livers
2 shallots
6½ tbsp/100 ml port
⅔ cup/150 ml heavy
  cream
6 tbsp butter
4 slices whole-grain
  bread
salt and pepper

Serves 4
Preparation time: 25 minutes
Cooking time: 15 minutes
Difficulty: ✶

1. Carefully clean the livers, removing the nerves and gall bladders. Sear the livers in a pan with some butter. Salt and pepper lightly.

2. Peel and chop the shallots. Stir them into the livers and brown a few minutes.

This cheerful and delicious dish is often served at buffets on crackers. This recipe, however, calls for large slices of toast, making it a more substantial appetizer.

Any kind of poultry liver will do, or you can try rabbit livers, which are equally succulent. When cleaning the livers, be careful not to break the gall bladder; its bitterness would ruin the whole dish.

The color of the sauce is important for your presentation. Do not add too much cream; the sauce should remain dark. It should also be thick, so it will have to reduce a fairly long time.

These canapés can be accompanied by a small salad, fresh and crisp, for a nice contrast with the livers.

A robust white Tursan, with its aroma of pine forests, will provide an ideal accompaniment to the canapés.

3. Pour in the port and simmer for about 30 seconds. Remove the livers and keep them warm.

4. Reduce the port to ⅔ its initial volume, then stir in the cream. Adjust the seasoning. Reduce further, until the liquid has evaporated by half.

Liver Canapés

5. Whisk in the butter, return the livers to the sauce, and bring it to a boil. Cook for 1 or 2 additional minutes.

6. Toast the bread and cover each slice with liver. Reduce the sauce again and nap it over the canapés. Serve with a small, slightly tart salad.

Shellfish with

1. Steam open the scallops, mussels, and clams, and remove the meat from the shells. Boil the periwinkles and let cool. Pour the cooking water through a strainer and reduce it its initial volume by half.

Ingredients:
4 sea scallops
1 lb/500 g mussels
3½ oz/100 g periwinkles
10½ oz/300 g clams
8 littleneck clams
12 oysters
½ cucumber
3½ oz/100 g green beans
2 tomatoes
1 leek
4 mushrooms
several leaves Savoy
   cabbage
6½ tbsp/100 g butter
3½ tbsp/50 ml vermouth
6½ tbsp/100 ml heavy
   cream
juice of ½ lemon
salt and pepper

Serves 6
Preparation time: 40 minutes
Cooking time: 15 minutes
Difficulty: ✶✶

This is a seafood lover's delight!

Because cabbage has such a strong flavor, only a few leaves are necessary. Otherwise, the cabbage might overpower the more delicate flavor of the shellfish.

To open the clams, place them in cold, salted water. In the process of cooking, they will cleanse themselves of their sand. Soak the scallops in very cold water to tenderize and blanch them.

The liquid in which the seafood is cooked will serve as the basis for the sauce. For this reason, it should not be seasoned until the end of the preparations. A bouquet garni, however, may be added early on. It is very important not to brown any of the vegetables, especially the leek. The sauce is white and must stay in harmony with its ingredients.

There are numerous varieties of shellfish, and you will be delighted to regale your guests with this unparalleled treasure from the sea.

Our wine expert suggests a Pouilly-Fumé (Domaine Ladoucette), which picks up a light hint of the sea in its Loire Valley vinyards.

2. Peel the cucumber and carve out small balls with a paring knife. Snap the string beans. Peel, seed, and dice the tomatoes. Julienne the leek and mushrooms. Once the periwinkles have cooled, remove them from their shells. Remove the oysters from their shells.

3. Boil two pots of water. Poach the cabbage in one, the green beans in the other. Lightly sauté the leek in a pan with some butter.

4. Add more butter and the remaining vegetables and sauté without letting them brown. Salt and pepper lightly. When tender, remove from heat and arrange on a serving dish.

Lemon-Butter Sauce

5. Pour the vermouth into the pan, reduce it, and add the reduced seafood cooking liquid. Stir in the cream, add the lemon juice, and simmer until thickened.

6. Arrange the vegetables on a warm platter. Swirl the butter into the sauce and nap it over the vegetables. Slice the scallops and garnish the platter with the seafood. Serve very warm.

Old-Fashioned

1. In a pot of slightly salted water, boil the sweetbreads and rooster kidneys for 10 minutes, and the cockscomb for 1 hour. Peel and julienne the carrot, then poach it in lightly salted water. Peel the cooked cockscomb.

Ingredients:

14 oz/400 g veal
   sweetbreads
8 rooster kidneys
4 rooster cockscomb
1 veal kidney
2 carrots
10 tbsp/150 g butter
5¼ oz/150 g mushrooms
5¼ oz/150 g oyster
   mushrooms
3½ oz/100 g *trompettes
   de la mort* mushrooms
6½ tbsp/100 ml vermouth
1 cube veal bouillon
1⅔ cups/400 ml heavy
   cream
10½ oz/300 g spinach
juice of ½ lemon
salt and pepper

Serves 4
Preparation time: 45 minutes
Cooking time: 50 minutes
Difficulty: ✶✶✶

A *beuchelle* is a light ragoût traditionally made from veal kidneys and sweetbreads, and rooster kidneys and cockscomb. This dish is a splendid regional specialty. Most people have never eaten cockscomb, unless they come from the area around Tourangelle. If you have trouble finding rooster kidneys, and in particular cockscomb, white chicken meat can be substituted. If you are able to find cockscomb, be aware that it must be very thoroughly cooked in order to develop its best flavor. Test the cockscomb for doneness with a knife: If it is easy to cut into, then it has cooked sufficiently.

A veal stock is a perfect sauce for this dish. If you do not have enough time to prepare it, add a bouquet garni to the cooking water with a chopped carrot and onion and cook for about one hour.. The sweetbreads should be seared in a very hot pan in a generous amount of butter.

Try a Vouvray Sec or Moelleux (Domaine G. Huet). These are among the best French wines, known for their delicate blend of honey and quince.

2. Remove the nerve from the veal kidney and cut the kidney in small pieces. Sear the pieces in a pan with some oil and a little butter. Set aside in a strainer. Brown the sweetbreads in butter in a separate pan.

3. Trim the stems from the various kinds of mushrooms, julienne the caps, and set aside. Slice the sweetbreads.

4. Pour the vermouth into a saucepan, and add the bouillon cube dissolved in ¾ cup/200 ml water. Stir in the cream and reduce the liquid to half its initial volume.

Beuchelle Tourangelle

5. Add the variety meats and simmer for a few more minutes. Steam the spinach in a little butter.

6. Add the mushrooms to this mixture and heat for a few minutes. Place the spinach in the center of a serving dish. Arrange the kidneys, sweetbread and cockscomb around it. Whisk the butter into the sauce, add lemon juice if desired, and decorate with julienned carrot.

Eggplant

1. Peel and finely chop the onion and the garlic. Cube the tomatoes.

Ingredients:
1 onion
1 clove of garlic
6 tomatoes
6½ tbsp/100 ml olive
   oil
1 bouquet garni
1 cup/250 ml water
2.2 lbs/1 kg eggplant
2 oz/50 g grated
   Parmesan
salt and pepper

Serves 6
Preparation time: 15 minutes
Cooking time: 35 minutes
Difficulty: ✲

2. Sauté the onion slowly in a little olive oil.

The eggplant is a vegetable in a class by itself. Its shiny, dark purple skin gives it a visual beauty that rivals its taste. It can be stuffed, sautéed, baked in a soufflé or, perhaps most commonly, stewed in a ratatouille. Some say that the eggplant originated in India and did not reach France until the seventeenth century. Though its season in France extends from May to October, it has become a year-round staple. It is low in calories and rich in potassium and calcium.

Eggplant is usually easy to handle, but it will soak up oil when sautéed. To lighten the eggplant, blot the excess grease with a paper towel. For the true flavor of the south of France, sauté it in olive oil mixed, if you like, with vegetable oil. When baked, the eggplant will release any excess oil. Pour this off before adding the cheese.

A good addition to this dish is zucchini. Slice the zucchini and alternate the zucchini with slices of eggplant. Though the tomatoes make this dish similar to ratatouille, the gratin allows the vegetables to shine forth in a different light. It is an excellent accompaniment to lamb chops or steak, or fish in the summer months.

Our wine expert insists that a white Montlouis, an ideal companion to vegetables, is the best choice for this meal.

3. Add the tomato, bouquet garni, and the garlic to the pan. Let simmer; season with salt and pepper. Add a glassful of water and simmer, covered, for about 20 minutes.

4. Purée the tomatoes with a food mill or food processor. Bring the purée to a boil. Adjust the seasoning and set aside.

au Gratin

5. Wash the eggplant and slice it thinly.

6. Fry the eggplant slices in olive oil; lightly salt and pepper. Spread tomato purée in the bottom of a baking dish and cover with a layer of eggplant slices. Repeat, ending with a final layer of eggplant. Bake the gratin for 10 minutes at 350 °F. Sprinkle with Parmesan cheese and serve.

Snail Turnovers

1. Thinly roll out the pastry and cut out 4 circles with a diameter of 6 in/15 cm. Place about half a dozen snails on each circle.

Ingredients:
1¼ lbs/600 g puff pastry (see basic recipe)
2 dozen snails
1 egg
1 bulb of garlic, peeled and chopped
1⅔ cups/400 ml heavy cream
3 egg yolks
3½ oz/100 ml unsweetened *crème chantilly*
salt and pepper

Serves 4
Preparation time: 20 minutes
Cooking time: 30 minutes
Difficulty: ✶

2. Beat the egg and lightly brush it around the edges of each circle. Fold the pastry over the snails and press firmly so that the layers stick together. Bake at 350 °F for 20 minutes.

This is a new version of an old classic—the turnover filled with snails in place of the more traditional apple. Our chef recommends *petit-gris* snails, available fresh from April to June, but canned or frozen snails will also do.

The turnovers are served with an extremely rich cream sauce that remains light in texture due to the addition of *crème chantilly*, a melodious name for whipped cream. *Crème chantilly* usually refers to cream sweetened with vanilla or liqueuer, whipped and used in desserts, but in this case no sugar should be added. Also, the garlic should not be left in the cream for more than five minutes or it will become unpleasantly acidic. If the garlic should be somewhat old, be sure to remove any green sprouts.

These turnovers are both filling and paradoxically appetizing. They are also rich in magnesium and vitamin C.

This hot entrée requires some extra effort, but you will be justly rewarded later, when you can relax and enjoy the turnovers.

A good white wine will delicately strengthen the flavor of the pastry while blending it with the snail filling. Open a Chablis Les Clos.

3. Peel and finely chop the garlic.

4. Bring the heavy cream just to a simmer. Add salt and pepper and stir in the minced garlic.

with Garlic Sauce

5. Add the yolks to the warm cream, stirring vigorously.

6. Lower the heat and gently blend the whipped cream into the sauce. Serve the turnovers with the sauce.

Carp in Reuilly

1. Peel and slice the shallots; peel and dice the carrot. Gently sauté them in ⅓ of the butter with the bacon.

Ingredients:
2 fillets of carp
4 shallots
1 carrot
10 tbsp/150 g butter
3½ oz/100 g unsliced
    smoked bacon
10½ oz/300 g puff
    pastry (see basic
    recipe)
1 tbsp flour
1 egg
1 bouquet garni
3 cups/750 ml Pinot
    noir de Reuilly
5 anchovy fillets
salt and pepper

Serves 4
Preparation time: 30 minutes
Cooking time: 20 minutes
Difficulty: ✴✴

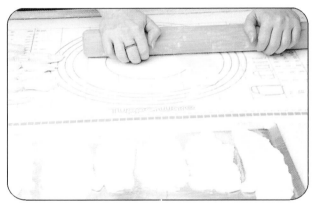

2. Prepare and roll out the puff pastry, using a little flour to keep it from sticking to the rolling pin or work surface. Cut out 15 slices and bake them at 400 °F for 2-3 minutes.

Beginning in the Middle Ages, carp was a fish served only to kings. Found in fresh quiet waters, its tongue was considered a particular delicacy.

Carp are available almost year-round; look for large, fresh fish. They are easiest to find between April and June. During the breeding season they will have neither eggs nor roe. You can also try pike or perch.

If the carp has just been caught, soak it in water with a little vinegar added after gutting and scaling it. This will cleanse it of its murky taste. Because the anchovy butter is already salty, be careful not to add too much salt during preparation.

This is an easy, straightforward recipe. You can save some time by buying prepared puff pastry or by making it in advance. Be sure to roll the pastry out very thinly so that it bakes into crisp slices.

Since carp is a freshwater fish, it should be served with red wine. Our wine expert recommends the same wine used in the recipe, a red Reuilly.

3. Once the vegetables and bacon have browned well, add the bouquet garni to the pan and stir in the red wine. Lightly salt and pepper and let simmer for 15 minutes.

4. To make the anchovy butter, combine the remaining butter with the anchovy fillets. Remove the vegetables from their pan and pour the cooking liquid through a strainer into a separate pan. Add the anchovy butter, bring just to a boil, and immediately remove from the heat.

Pinot Sauce

5. Thinly slice the carp. Salt and pepper the fillets and sauté them in a pan for 30 seconds on each side.

6. On a serving dish, alternate the pastry slices with the fish. Bring the sauce to a boil and adjust its seasoning. Pour the sauce around the fish and pastry, and serve very hot.

Shallot

1. Peel and chop the shallots.

Ingredients:
10 shallots
2 cups/500 ml milk
6 eggs
salt and pepper

Serves 5
Preparation time: 15 minutes
Cooking time: 30 minutes
Difficulty: ★★

2. Bring the milk to a boil, add the shallots, and let this simmer a few minutes.

The shallot is a member of the same family as onions and garlic; its flavor, however, is more subtle than onion and less acid than garlic. Shallots have been cultivated for two thousand years. Today, the shallot is considered a culinary treasure and its sweet flavor refines any sauce, however plain.

Finely chop the shallots, using a food processor if necessary. Be careful to sauté them over low heat. When you add the warm milk and shallots to the eggs, beat vigorously to prevent the eggs from cooking in the heat.

This recipe calls for you to strain the mixture to remove the shallots. If you prefer to keep the shallots in the flan, skip this step. Let the flan cool before trying to unmold it. Once it is cold, run a knife between the mold and the flan, gently tap the mold and the flan should come out easily and in one piece.

You can vary this recipe by using different vegetables such as nettles, spinach, fennel, carrots, zucchini, or turnips. Cook the vegetables before adding them to the milk. Also try making small, individual-size flans; dinner guests always enjoy them. A Pouilly-Fumé will beautifully underscore the shallot's sweet undertones.

3. When the shallots are done, break the eggs into a bowl and beat vigorously.

4. When the eggs are foamy, add salt and pepper and beat one more minute.

Flan

5. Pour the milk and shallots onto the eggs, stirring vigorously.

6. Pass this mixture through a strainer to remove the shallots, then pour the liquid into a pre-buttered mold. Bake in a bain-marie for 30 minutes at 350 °F. Serve warm.

Zucchini and

1. Halve and slice the zucchini and cook them in slightly salted boiling water until tender.

Ingredients:
1¾ lbs/800 g zucchini
2 eggs
1 shallot
1 laurel leaf
1 sprig of thyme
1 clove of garlic
½ cup/125 ml dry
   white wine
16 clams
6½ tbsp/100 ml
   crème fraîche
4 tsp/20 g softened
   butter
salt and pepper

Serves 4
Preparation time: 20 minutes
Cooking time: 30 minutes
Difficulty: ✲

2. Strain the zucchini well and purée in a food mill or processor.

Zucchini is traditionally most often found in Mediterranean cooking, though in the past fifty years, it has made its way north and, indeed, around the world. There are several varieties of zucchini, all of which are available year-round. Our chef likes the "diamond" zucchini, which is fairly small and narrow. It has a delicate taste and an excellent consistency—it also happens to be the most readily available.

Clams are also not difficult to find, though you may substitute mussels if you prefer. The sauce used here has no flour, so it remains very light; the butter adds extra flavor but could also be omitted. Zucchini itself is very low in calories, so this is a healthful, light dish. It can be reheated easily and the cooked zucchini can be kept in the refrigerator for up to three days.

Our wine expert feels that a Muscadet sur lie, with its undertones of the sea, is the perfect wine to serve with this meal.

3. Beat the eggs and stir them into the zucchini purée. Add salt and pepper.

4. Whip the purée and adjust the seasoning. Butter small ramekins and fill them with the purée. Bake them for 20 minutes at 300 °F in a bain-marie.

Clam Mousse

5. While the zucchini is baking, chop the shallot and place it in a pot with the laurel, thyme, and garlic. Pour in the wine land bring to a boil.

6. Steam the clams in this broth. Once they have opened, remove the clams from their shell. Pour the broth through a strainer and reduce it by half. Stir in the crème fraîche. Reduce a few more minutes, then whisk in the butter. Unmold the mousse and serve with the clams and sauce.

Fennel Pie

1. Marinate the 4 fish fillets in a mixture of the white wine and 1 tbsp olive oil seasoned with salt, pepper and celery salt. Slice the shallots thinly and add to the marinade.

2. Cube the fennel, blanch it for 2 minutes, drain and allow to cool. Pour the rest of the oil into a pot and sauté the fennel. Add salt, pepper, and basil.

3. Roll the pastry dough out into 2 large pieces. Ease one into a cake pan and prick the bottom with a fork. Once the fennel has cooled, place half of it on the dough.

Ingredients:

1 fillet of each:
   mackerel, sea bass,
   bream, and goatfish
1 cup/250 ml dry
   white wine
6½ tbsp/100 ml olive
   oil
1 pinch of celery salt
2 shallots
3 bulbs of fennel
8 leaves of basil,
   chopped
1 lb/500 g puff pastry
   (see basic recipe)
1 egg
⅔ cup/150 ml heavy
   cream
salt and pepper

Serves 6
Preparation time: 1 hour
Cooking time: 55 minutes
Difficulty: ✷✷

Loving fennel? This recipe is full of the kinds of surprising twists and turns that recall true love.

In ancient times, pies were not only sweet and salty pies such as this held an important place in the kitchen, either as an appetizer or a main course. Unfortunately, they were eventually replaced by individual pastries. This recipe restores the savory pie to its former place of honor.

Our chef stresses the importance of blanching the fennel before using it, to remove its bitter taste. Omitting this step could ruin the dish.

This pie can be reheated or eaten cold. It can also be kept in the refrigerator for up to three days.

Our chef also suggests varying this recipe by whipping the cream with a little lemon and spooning it onto the serving platter with a pinch of celery salt—really a delicacy.

The aroma of the fennel will go well with a Chablis.

4. Remove the fish fillets from the marinade and lay them on the fennel. Beat the egg and brush it along the edge of the pastry.

Amoureuse

5. Scatter the remaining fennel on top of the fish and cover with the second layer of pastry. Pinch the edges to seal and cut off excess dough. Bake for 30 minutes at 350 °F.

6. While the pie is baking, reduce the marinade to ¾ its original volume. Stir in the cream, season with salt and pepper, and allow to thicken over low heat. Pour the sauce through a strainer and serve with the pie.

Crab Ravioli with

1. Peel and dice the onion, carrot, and celery. Sauté them in 1 tbsp oil. Add the blue crabs and combine well. Cover and set aside for 10 minutes.

Ingredients:
1 small onion, 1 carrot
2 celery stalks
1¾ lbs/800 g blue crabs
3½ tbsp/50 ml cognac
3½ tbsp/50 ml port
1 cup/250 ml fish stock
  (see basic recipe)
1 cup/250 ml white wine
1¼ cups/300 ml heavy
  cream
1 clove garlic, chopped
4 tsp/20 ml tomato paste
1 pinch cayenne pepper
1⅓ cups/160 g flour
1 tbsp corn starch
4½ oz/125 g snow or king
  crabmeat
1 tbsp/15 g butter
salt and pepper

Serves 4
Preparation time: 35 minutes
Cooking time: 45 minutes
Difficulty: ✷✷

Cousins of the Italian ravioli, these little filled pockets are traditional fare in Corsica and the area around Nice. When you cut the circles out of the pasta dough, take care not to let the edges get too wet or they will open while cooking. To close them, firmly press the sides together so that they stay sealed. This is probably the most crucial step in preparing this dish.

Remember to butter the utensil used to steam the ravioli to prevent them from sticking and then tearing apart.

Blue crabs are very easy to catch. Their flesh is very flavorful and will lend a wonderful taste to the sauce, which in fact is very easy to prepare. Simply cut each crab in quarters with a knife and remove the meat.

Our wine expert never fails to suggest amazing wines: Try a Château de Crémat (Bellet blanc). Situated high above the French Riviera, this tiny winery produces delicate wines with linden undertones.

2. Pour in the cognac and port and flambé it. Pour in the fish stock and stir in the white wine and cream. Now add the garlic, tomato paste, and pinch of cayenne pepper. Let simmer for 30 minutes over low heat.

3. For the pasta dough, combine the flour and corn starch, then stir in ⅔ cup/150 ml boiling water and mix thoroughly.

4. Roll out the pasta dough thinly and cut out circles with a diameter of 2 in/5 cm. Place a small amount of king or snow crab meat on each circle. Lightly dampen the edges of each portion.

Blue Crab Sauce

5. Close the pasta crescents, pinching the edges together firmly. Remove the blue crab meat from the shells and purée together with the vegetables and marinade. Pass the mixture through a strainer and adjust the seasoning, if necessary.

6. Steam the ravioli and then sauté them quickly in a little butter. Pour the sauce on a serving platter and arrange the raviolis on it; serve warm.

Lobster and

1. Boil the lobster in water with the onion, carrot, bouquet garni, and vinegar.

Ingredients:
1 2-lb/900-g lobster
1 onion, cubed
1 carrot, sliced
1 bouquet garni
2 tbsp/30 ml vinegar
7 oz/200 g whiting
2 eggs
¾ cup/200 ml heavy
    cream
10 basil leaves
salt and pepper

Serves 4
Preparation time: 25 minutes
Cooking time: 35 minutes
Difficulty: ✶✶

2. Fillet and skin the whiting (see basic recipe). Remove as many of the bones as possible, then blend the fillets in a food processor. Add the eggs and blend again.

When all is said and done, the lobster is simply one of the tastiest products of the sea. It was once plentiful along the coast of Brittany, though it is much more difficult to find in France today. Along the northern coasts of North America, however, the lobster is still abundant. Lobster flesh is at the samt time low in calories and high in minerals, such as phosphorus and potassium.

This recipe works equally well with crabmeat, if that is your preference.

For the proper mousse consistency, the fish should be very cold when you purée it. It should also be heavily salted to remove excess moisture and help the meat stay firm.

This warm appetizer, healthful and easy to prepare, can also be served as an entrée. Leeks and spinach make good accompanying vegetables. The flan can be reheated but should not be kept for more than 24 hours.

To add the final touch, try a great wine: Puligny-Montrachet Les Folatières.

3. Season the mousse with salt, and blend in the cream.

4. Add the basil leaves to the mousse and purée until homogenous.

Basil Flan

5. Remove all the lobster meat from the shell. Dice the meat and chop the roe finely. Add the roe to the mousse.

6. Line a ramekin with the mousse. Add the cubed lobster and cover with another layer of mousse. Bake in a bain-marie for 20 minutes at 350 °F. Serve warm with a beurre blanc (see basic recipe).

Skate Fins

1. Groove the surface of the zucchini and carrots so they are striped. Cut the carrots at a slant, slice the zucchini thinly, and julienne the peppers.

2. Divide the sugar and vinegar evenly into 3 separate pots. Bring them to a boil and let simmer for 5 minutes.

Ingredients:
2 skate fins
1 lb/500 g short pastry
   (see basic recipe)
For the pickled
   vegetables:
8¾ oz/250 g zucchini
8¾ oz/250 g carrots
4 cups/500 g sugar
¾ cup/200 ml vinegar
4¼ oz/120 g red bell
   pepper
2 limes
For the mousse:
7 oz/200 g freshwater
   codfish
2 eggs
¾ cup/200 ml crème
   fraîche
salt and pepper

Serves 4
Preparation time: 25 minutes
Cooking time: 45 minutes
Difficulty: ✳✳✳

Skate is a cartilaginous fish found in both warm and cool waters. It has no bones and the cartilage is easy to remove. Many varieties exist, but the most common and also the most delicious is the one whose gray stripes give it the appearance of marble. They often grown to be as wide as 50 inches (120 centimeters)!

When skate is fresh, it secretes a viscous liquid that will continue to appear up to 10 hours after the skate dies. This is a good way to test the fish's freshness: If you wipe off the liquid and it does not reappear, the skate may not be very fresh.

Skate has a unique taste that goes well with the sweet and vinegary flavors of this dish. There is no way to ruin the mousse as long as the fish is very cold—in fact, all the ingredients used to make the mousse should be very cold— and you avoid overbeating. This recipe is fairly difficult to prepare; it is also time-consuming. However, it is worth the time and effort. Please note that the most difficult step is pickling the vegetables.

This dish should be served as soon as it is removed from the oven. It can be rewarmed in the microwave.

The sharpness of a Muscadet sur lie will go well with the vinegar overtones in this dish.

3. Put the zucchini in one pot, the carrots in another, and the peppers and the quartered limes in the third. Simmer until the vegetables become slightly transparent.

4. Poach the skate in a court-bouillon (see basic recipe). Combine the chilled codfish and the eggs in a food processor to create a mousse. Season with salt and pepper, and whisk in the crème fraîche. Beat until smooth.

with Vegetables

5. Prepare the puff pastry, then roll it out evenly and use it to line the baking dishes. Cover with a layer of fish mousse and top with the cooled skate.

6. Cover with the pickled vegetables. Close with the top layer of pastry. Bake at 400 °F for 20 minutes. Serve the pie warm with beurre blanc (see basic recipe).

Potato and

1. Peel and cube the potatoes. Blanch them lightly in boiling water. Drain and let cool.

Ingredients:
2.2 lbs/1 kg potatoes
10½ oz/300
    mushrooms
3 cloves of garlic
thyme
laurel
nutmeg, grated
1 cup/250 ml milk
1 cup/250 ml crème
    fraîche
1¾ oz/50 g grated
    Gruyère cheese
salt and pepper

Serves 6
Preparation time: 15 minutes
Cooking time: 20 minutes
Difficulty: ✶

2. Clean and finely dice the mushrooms.

Potatoes seem so plain, yet they can be used in an infinite number of ways and remain a tasty and ever popular vegetable. Their virtues are likewise seemingly endless: they contain glucose, protein, minerals, iron, iodine, water, and vitamins B & C. New potatoes are especially rich in vitamin C.

This gratin makes a wonderful side dish for a meat entrée.

The garlic cream in which the potatoes and mushrooms are cooked impart a superb flavor to the vegetables.

Serve this gratin as soon as the top darkens. Should there be any leftover, it can also be reheated in the oven or microwave.

Your choice of wine depends on the meat served with the gratin. But a Graves should suit the meat being served, whatever the choice, especially since both red and white wines are produced.

3. Lightly boil the mushrooms. Season with a little salt and pepper.

4. Bring the milk to a boil and add the garlic, thyme, laurel, and grated nutmeg. Add a little salt and pepper.

Mushroom Gratin

5. Add the potatoes to the milk and stir in the crème fraîche. Let simmer for 10 minutes.

6. Stir in the mushrooms. Pour the mixture into a buttered baking dish. Sprinkle with the grated cheese and broil for 5 minutes. Serve warm.

Creamed

1. Peel the carrots and boil them in slightly salted water until tender.

Ingredients:
2.2 lbs/1 kg carrots
⅔ cup/150 ml heavy
 cream
2¾ oz/80 g grated
 Gruyère cheese
10½ oz/300 g fresh
 spinach
⅓ cup/80 g butter
salt and pepper

Serves 6
Preparation time: 10 minutes
Cooking time: 20 minutes
Difficulty: ✳

2. Grind the carrots in a food mill or processor.

People have attributed nutritional values to carrots for centuries. Probably the most common bit of carrot lore is that they are good for your eyesight. Interestingly, however, carrots were not eaten commonly until the Renaissance. Until then they were just another root vegetable. In fact, they did not begin to acquire their trademark orange color until the mid-nineteenth century.

Today the carrot is a year-round delight. New carrots are the best available, especially those grown in Crèances near the English Channel. And carrots are, after all, a very nutritious food—they are rich in water, sugar, minerals, pectin, vitamins, and especially pro-vitamin A.

This excellent purée will be a fantastic accompaniment for any main course, meat or fish. The sweet taste of the carrot and the unctuousness of the cream calls for a dry Chablis.

3. Drain off any water and evaporate excess moisture over low heat, stirring continuously.

4. Pour on the heavy cream and stir vigorously.

Carrots

5. Stir the grated cheese into the carrot mixture. Clean and lightly blanch the spinach.

6. Add the butter to the carrots and stir vigorously. Adjust the seasoning if necessary. Serve with the blanched spinach leaves.

Muenster and

1. Prepare the puff pastry, chill it, then roll it out evenly and sprinkle with flour.

Ingredients:
14 oz/400 g puff
    pastry (see basic
    recipe)
flour for dusting
12½ oz/350 g
    Muenster cheese
1 bunch of chives
1 egg
1 pinch of cumin
3 tbsp crème fraîche
salt and pepper

Serves 4
Preparation time: 15 minutes
Cooking time: 20 minutes
Difficulty: ✳

2. Cut the piece of Muenster into 4 wedges of approximately equal size.

The history of cheese is as long as the history of farming. It was the staple of farming families' diet for centuries, but local methods of cheese-making have produced a tremendous variety of cheeses and a myriad of uses for them. Rich in protein, calcium, and phosphorus, cheese contains everything needed for healthy growth.

Muenster cheese was probably first made by monks in the Alsation region, and hence derives its name from the word "monastery." Its reputation spread quickly throughout France. It is a typical Alsatian cow's milk cheese with a soft rind covering an often soft and creamy interior, and though its flavor is usually mild, it bears no resemblance to the quite bland Munster cheese common in the United States. Its only drawback, for those who are sensitive, is its strong odor. Similar cheeses can be substituted for the Muenster, such as a Maroilles, Pont-l'évêque, or Roblechon.

The puff pastry can be made in advance and frozen. Try brushing egg yolk over each serving to make the crust more attractive. A good garden salad sprinkled with nuts will make an excellent accompaniment.

Our wine expert offers an unexpected suggestion: a Gerwurztraminer.

3. Chop the chives and set them aside.

4. Cut out pastry triangles 2-3 times the size of each wedge of cheese. Brush the edge of the pastry with the beaten egg and set a cheese wedge in the middle of each piece. Fold the pastry over the cheese, pressing the edges firmly to seal.

Cumin Turnovers

5. Brush the tops of the pastry with egg and sprinkle with the cumin. Bake at 350 °F for 20 minutes.

6. In a bowl, combine the cream with the chives. Salt and pepper to taste. Whip the cream until smooth and serve with the warm turnovers.

Sautéed Veal

1. Soak the sweetbreads in water overnight. Slice and press them to flatten.

2. Sprinkle the sweetbreads with salt and pepper, then with flour, and set them aside on a dish towel.

Ingredients:
2.2 lbs/1 kg veal
    sweetbreads
flour for dredging
6½ tbsp/100 ml oil
trompette de la morte
    mushrooms
salt and pepper
For the garlic sauce:
6 cloves of garlic
1 cube chicken
    bouillon
¾ cup/200 ml crème
    fraîche
1 tbsp butter
For the tomato sauce:
2 shallots
1 tbsp butter
4 tomatoes
1 bouquet garni

Serves 5
Preparation time: 35 minutes
Cooking time: 25 minutes
Difficulty: ✶✶

This simple recipe takes little time to prepare. Fresh and colorful, original and appetizing, it will satisfy everyone. Tomatoes—rich in water, low in calories, and full of vitamins A, B, and C— are one of its most important ingredients.

Garlic has a long and happy history—apparently both the Egyptians and the Romans ate it to build up their strength. Today, it is enjoying something of a renaissance as a medicinal food. Some people even swear garlic will help you live longer.

When cooked in its skin, garlic takes on a slightly nutty flavor that is very different from its perhaps more familiar taste when peeled. You may or may not choose to peel the garlic in Step 3, but our chef does recommend removing the green core of the garlic, if present, in any case.

This dish should cook very slowly. If the broth reduces too quickly, the bouillon cube may oversalt the sauce and the garlic will not be done.

Our wine expert suggests a Puligny-les-Pucelles.

3. Peel and halve the garlic cloves, removing any green sprouts in the core. Peel the shallots and chop them finely. Seed and chop the tomatoes.

4. Dissolve the bouillon cube in 6½ tbsp/100 ml boiling water. Add the garlic and let simmer. In a separate pot, make the tomato sauce: Sauté the shallots in the butter. Stir in the tomatoes and bouquet garni. Season with salt and pepper.

Sweetbreads

5. Brown the sweetbreads in the oil over low heat, turning them occasionally.

6. Remove the bouquet garni and blend the tomato sauce with a hand mixer. Add the crème fraîche to the garlic fond and blend until smooth, then whisk in the remaining butter. Arrange the sweetbreads on a platter with the 2 sauces. Garnish with trompette de la mort mushrooms, and serve hot.

Veal Liver with

1. Clean the asparagus, cut them in half, and boil in slightly salted water. Cut off the tips and set aside. Carefully clean the parsley and discard the stems.

Ingredients:
20 asparagus
1 bunch of parsley
1 cube chicken
  bouillon
¾ cup/200 ml water
3½ tbsp/50 g butter
flour
4 slices (or 2 thick
  slices) veal liver
6½ tbsp/100 ml
  cooking oil
salt and pepper

Serves 4
Preparation time: 20 minutes
Cooking time: 35 minutes
Difficulty: ✶✶

2. Dissolve the bouillon cube in the water. Make a beurre manié from 1 tbsp of butter and an equal amount of flour, add it to the bouillon, and stir the sauce until smooth.

The reputation of many a fine restaurant rests on the ways in which it prepares and serves liver. The fine flavor of liver is a favorite medium for the creative chef.

Parsley also has an interesting place in culinary history. Legend has it that Hercules, after vanquishing the lion, placed a crown of parsley on his head, and Greek poets supposedly placed parsley on their heads for inspiration. Aesculapius, moreover, taught Achilles the healing power of parsley.

In this recipe the parsley is fried, which gives it a fantastic crunch. Be sure to place the fried parsley on a paper towel to drain off any excess grease.

Our chef suggests you choose small wild asparagus, when in season. These are usually found in the spring. Not only are they very attractive, but they also have a light almond flavor. Be careful handling the fragile tips.

A Pinot Gris Tokay will be a good wine to serve with this dish.

3. Set aside half the parsley. Blanch the other half and then refresh it, reserving the cooking water. Dry the parsley and purée it in a blender. Reduce the cooking liquid by half, then stir it into the bouillon and bring to a boil. Blend the sauce again. Adjust the seasoning and whip in half of the butter.

4. Sprinkle the liver slices with flour, season with salt and pepper, and set aside.

Parsley and Asparagus

5. Sprinkle the asparagus with flour and sauté in a pan with a little butter.

6. Briefly fry the reserved parsley in oil. Remove and drain the parsley, add a little butter to the pan, and sauté the veal liver. Bring the sauce to a boil; blend it briefly before serving to give it volume and adjust the seasoning. Serve the livers with the sauce, asparagus, and fried parsley.

Asparagus

1. Peel the mushrooms and clean them carefully. Simmer them in a cup of slightly salted water with the lemon juice and 1 tbsp of butter.

Ingredients:
8¾ oz/250 g
  mushrooms
juice of ½ lemon
¾ cup/200 g butter
1 bunch of asparagus
  (approx. 1 lb/500 g)
2 egg yolks
1 cup/250 ml crème
  fraîche
salt and pepper

Serves 4
Preparation time: 25 minutes
Cooking time: 20 minutes
Difficulty: ✲✲

2. Peel the asparagus. Tie them together and poach in slightly salted boiling water. Remove them while still crisp and refresh under cold water.

There is nothing quite like asparagus in season. As old as ancient Egypt, asparagus did not arrive in France until the seventeenth century, and then it was reserved exclusively for the royal table.

To maintain the white color of the mushrooms as they boil, they should be moistened with a little lemon juice.

The key to a successful Hollandaise sauce is to beat the egg yolks vigorously while they warmed in the top of a double boiler. The sauce should have the lightness of a mousse, and be perfectly smooth. Continue beating until the last drop of butter has been added and the entire sauce has cooled.

Do not forget to plunge the asparagus in cold water after blanching it to halt the cooking process. This will help preserve its color and flavor. If you like your asparagus crisp, try steaming instead of blanching. You might also try replacing the Hollandaise sauce with a sabayon sauce, which is simply egg yolks and milk added to the mushrooms. Broil it briefly, and the sabayon will be done.

Our wine expert is caught up in the ebullience and lushness of springtime, and therefore suggests serving a Xérès Fino.

3. Melt the remaining butter. In the top of a double boiler beat the egg yolks together with a drop of water until creamy and light. Blend the cooked mushrooms in a food processor, and gradually add the butter sabayon to them.

4. Continue to add the butter sabayon, whipping constnatly until a homogenous Hollandaise sauce is formed. Whip the crème fraîche until foamy and somewhat stiff.

Gratin

5. Gently fold the whipped crème fraîche into the Hollandaise sauce. Arrange the asparagus on a serving platter.

6. Spoon the sauce over the asparagus and broil for a few minutes. Serve hot.

Veal Sweetbreads

1. Bring a pot of water to the boil. Peel and chop the onion, carrots, and celery and place them in the pot. Season with the thyme, lemon juice and salt and pepper. Poach the sweetbreads in this liquid for 20 minutes.

2. Dry the sweetbreads and let them cool. Then scallop them and lightly dredge with flour lightly seasoned with salt and pepper. Sauté in a pan with the butter and oil.

Ingredients:
1 onion
2 carrots
1 stalk of celery
1 sprig of thyme
juice of 1 lemon
2 veal sweetbreads
3 tbsp/25 g flour
1 tbsp/15 g butter
1 tbsp/15 ml oil
1 cup/250 ml port
1¾ oz/50 g freeze-
   dried morels
5 cups/1.25 liters
   light cream
salt and pepper

Serves 4
Preparation time: 15 minutes
Cooking time: 20 minutes
Difficulty: ✶

Veal and lamb sweetbreads are considered, with good reason, the most delicate of all organ meats. The precious morels, which bloom in the earth in the spring, are unfortunately growing ever more difficult to find, but their taste is wonderful and it is worth searching them out.

Soak the sweetbreads overnight in cold water with a little vinegar added to guarantee a white color when boiled. Be careful when handling the sweetbreads, for they are soft and fragile. Sauté them at low heat so they do not burn or stick to the pan.

Clean the morels carefully; they often have dirt hidden deep in their folds. They should be rinsed and soaked several times in different bowls of water before being added to the cream. They should also be patted dry to remove any excess moisture before cooking.

A great Château du Médoc, one of the best French wines, should accompany this classic French recipe. Try a Château Léoville-Las-Cases (St. Julien).

3. Drain any excess fat from the frying pan, then deglaze it with the port. Let this reduce for 1 minute at very low heat.

4. Reconstitute the morels in water, them trim their stems and rinse very carefully. Over low heat, simmer them in half of the cream. Add a little salt and pepper.

with Morels

5. Once the port has reduced, pour in the remaining cream and stir well to combine the juice left in the pan. Let this reduce for 2 minutes over low heat.

6. Pour the deglazed sauce through a strainer into the morel sauce, allowing the 2 to blend thoroughly. Spoon the sauce onto a warm platter, arrange the scallops, and serve hot.

Foie Gras

1. Peel the asparagus. Bring two pots of slightly salted water to a boil and poach the green asparagus in one and the wild asparagus in the other.

Ingredients:
14 oz/400 g green asparagus
1 bunch (approx. 1 lb/450 g) wild asparagus
5¼ oz/150 g porcini mushrooms
1 duck foie gras
10 tbsp/150 g butter
1⅔ cups/400 ml chicken or duck stock
3½ oz/100 g red currants
salt and pepper

Serves 6
Preparation time: 30 minutes
Cooking time: 20 minutes
Difficulty: ✲✲

2. While the asparagus is cooking, thinly slice the porcini. Cut the foie gras into thick slices and season with salt and pepper.

Fresh foie gras requires a good deal of attention, maybe even a moment of silence, before being eaten. It is such a delicate food that it deserves a clean and fresh palate to appreciate the full effect of its flavors. After you slice the foie gras, refrigerate it to keep it as cold as possible.

Always avoid serving a vegetable that is too strong to accompany foie gras. Asparagus is a perfect choice.

The proper wine to serve with foie gras has been a subject of controversy for years, and there is no end to the debate in sight. This leaves the decision up to you. Choose anything from the noble Château Yquem to a great white Bourgogne or even champagne. In no case, however, should you serve port, for it might well overshadow more subtle flavors. Try a classic Sauternes, such as a Château Suduiraut, or, as always, a Fino de Xérès to bring a touch of folly to your meal.

3. In a nonstick pan, sauté the foie gras for a few moments on each side.

4. In the same pan, sauté the asparagus slowly in some of the butter. Add salt and pepper and set aside.

with Asparagus Tips

5. Sauté the porcini, then deglaze the pan with the stock.

6. Stir the red currants into the mushrooms and pour some of the mixture onto a serving platter. Arrange the foie gras and asparagus on it, cover with the remaining sauce, and serve warm.

Crab Pouches

1. Poach the crab in the court-bouillon. When done, remove all the meat from the crab.

Ingredients:
1 large king or snow crab
court-bouillon (see basic recipe)
6½ tbsp/100 g butter
1 carrot
1 leek
1 zucchini
10 basil leaves
6 unsweetened crêpes (see basic recipe)
1 cup/250 ml crème fraîche
salt and pepper

Serves 3
Preparation time: 45 minutes
Cooking time: 25 minutes
Difficulty: ✳✳

2. Melt the butter in a saucepan. Add the chopped carrot, leek and zucchini; cover and let sweat at very low heat. Season with salt and pepper.

These puffy, blond pouches are filled with one of the best meats the ocean has to offer, though you may also substitute other varieties of crab or even lobster. Choose a large, heavy crab. Some cooks like to add a pinch of cayenne pepper in the cooking water when boiling the crab. Also, feel free to use a hammer to break the crab claws, but be sure that the crab has cooled, for it is easy to burn yourself.

To save time, make the crêpe batter the night before. This time-saving step will also make for a better crêpe since the batter improves with time.

The vegetables must sweat in a covered pan, and they should not be allowed to brown. Save some of the leek for tying the pockets together—blanch a few long strips of leek to use them as strings. Run cold water over them immediately after blanching to keep them from overcooking.

Do not place the pouches onto the sauce until the dish is ready to be served. If they are left for any length of time in the sauce, the crêpes will absorb liquid and disintigrate. This dish should be served warm and will not stand reheating. These special pouches demand a special wine: Our wine expert suggests the nutty flavor of roasted almonds in a Meursault Genevrières.

3. Gently stir the crab meat into the vegetables.

4. Chop the basil leaves and add half to the saucepan. Gently stir in 1 tbsp of the crème fraîche.

with Basil Sauce

5. Place a portion of the crab mixture in the center of each crêpe.

6. Tie each crêpe into a pouch with a strip of blanched leek. Reduce the remaining crème fraîche. Add a little salt and pepper and stir in the remaining basil. Let simmer a few minutes, then serve with the pouches.

Stuffed

1. Clean the mushrooms. Cut off the stems and scrape out the inside of the caps. Set aside the caps, stems, and scrapings.

Ingredients:
12 large mushrooms
2 shallots
6½ tbsp/100 g butter
36 snails
1 clove of garlic
1 bunch of chives
1 bunch of dill
1 bunch of chervil
¾ cup/200 ml crème fraîche
2 tomatoes
salt and freshly ground pepper

Serves 4
Preparation time: 30 minutes
Cooking time: 25 minutes
Difficulty: ✶✶

2. Finely chop the shallots and sauté them in butter. Chop the mushroom stems and scrapings and add to the shallots. Season with salt and pepper.

One of the nicest things about this recipe is that it uses plain, ordinary mushrooms. In France, these are called *champignons de Paris*. Their cultivation began during the Middle Ages, and under Napoleon they were widely grown in the 15th arrondissement of Paris, which was more or less deserted at the time: Hence their name. Choose mushrooms with large caps that will be easier to stuff. These mushrooms are rich in phosphorus and in vitamin B but low in calories.

Our chef recommends the *petit-gris* snails for their delicate, firm texture and fruity taste. The shallots should be sautéed thoroughly, and the mushroom caps should be delicately sautéed before baking. This dish can be reheated, but cannot be kept overnight.

A good white Bourgogne will go well with these delightful morsels. Our wine expert suggests a Chassagne-Montrachet.

3. Cut up the snails, and finely chop the garlic, chives, dill and chervil.

4. Once the mushrooms have dried out nicely, add half the chives and all the garlic. Stir in the dill and chervil. Add the snails to the mixture and allow to cook a few minutes.

Mushrooms

5. Stuff the mushroom caps with the sautéed filling. Place them in a baking dish with a little butter and bake at 350 °F for 15 minutes.

6. Bring the crème fraîche to a boil and season with a little salt and pepper. Stir in the remaining chives and the tomatoes. Once the mushrooms are done, pour the sauce onto a plate and arrange the mushrooms on top. Garnish with leftover herbs.

Bay Scallop-Filled

Ingredients:
4½ lbs/2 kg bay scallops (weight includes shell)
10½ oz/300 g shallots
13 tbsp/200 g butter
3 cups/750 ml red wine
1 bunch of dill
1 bunch of chervil
12 flowering zucchini
3½ oz/100 g cherry tomatoes
salt and pepper

Serves 4
Preparation time: 45 minutes
Cooking time: 40 minutes
Difficulty: ✴✴

1. Open the scallops and remove the meat. Clean thoroughly.

2. Chop the scallops into large dice and refrigerate.

Rose petals, chrysanthemums, magnolia blossoms, marjoram flowers, jasmine, nasturtium, violets and orange blossoms—in any country, in any time, gastronomy speaks a floral language. Fried zucchini blossoms come to us from the region of Nice, and our chef likes to serve them with seafood.

In order to save a bit of work, you may buy bay scallops already shelled, or you could try substituting sea scallops or crab.

Our chef suggests covering the zucchini blossoms with aluminum foil. This will allow the steam to rise and retain some moisture and flavor. Serve immediately after cooking; this dish cannot be reheated.

Our wine expert reminds us that tradition dictates serving the same wine used to prepare the dish. Therefore, one must use a wine of the ocean—a red Anjou is appropriate. Try a Château de Passavant.

3. Peel and chop the shallots. Sauté them lightly in butter, then pour in the wine. Stir and reduce to ¾ its original volume.

4. Chop the dill and chervil and combine them with the scallops. Add salt and pepper. Stir gently to cover all the scallops.

Zucchini Blossoms

5. Butter a baking dish. Sprinkle in the remaining herbs and carefully stuff the zucchini blossoms with the scallops. Pour a glass of salted water in the pan. Cover and steam over very low heat.

6. Pour the reduced wine through a strainer and bring to a boil. Whisk in the butter. Spoon this red butter sauce onto a serving dish, arrange the zucchini on the platter, and garnish with herbs.

Kidney with

1. Dissolve the bouillon cube in 8 cups/2 liters water. Add the chopped carrot, onion, celery, leek, parsley and salt and pepper. Simmer over low heat for 20 min-utes. Thinly slice the cabbage and blanch in slightly salted water, then refresh it in cold water and drain.

2. Clean the veal kidneys thoroughly and roll them tightly in plastic wrap.

Ingredients:
1 cube chicken bouillon
1 carrot
1 onion
1 celery stalk
1 leek
3 sprigs of parsley
1 Chinese cabbage
2 veal kidneys
3½ oz/100 g cockscomb
3½ oz/100 g rooster kidneys
10 tbsp/150 g butter
salt and pepper

Serves 4
Preparation time: 35 minutes
Cooking time: 55 minutes
Difficulty: ✶ ✶

You can find a wide variety of cabbages in any supermarket. This recipe will work best with either Chinese cabbage or savoy cabbage, though ultimately, the choice of cabbage depends on availability and is up to you.

Cockscomb is an unusual ingredient and can be difficult to find; you may have to special-order it from a local butcher. If it is unavailable, white chicken meat can be substituted. Cockscomb needs to cook for 35 to 45 minutes. They should remain tender, but it can be quite difficult to gauge their consistency.

The plastic wrap in which the kidneys are enveloped should be tied very tightly around them so that they are watertight while poaching. Some steam will form as the kidneys are immersed in the bouillon, but it should not be allowed to penetrate the plastic wrap. This would speed up the cooking time of the kidneys—something to avoid. Poach the kidneys for exactly twelve minutes. This will allow them to cook on the outside and remain slightly pink on the inside.

Discover with this dish a solid red wine from Bourgogne, which has gone unnoticed for too long: Monthélie.

3. Pour the bouillon through a strainer and bring to a boil. Poach the cockscomb in the bouillon for about 35 minutes. Add the rooster kidneys for an additional 10 minutes, then remove and drain the meats.

4. In the same bouillon, poach the veal kidneys in the plastic wrap for exactly 12 minutes.

Cockscomb

5. Unwrap the veal kidneys and slice them. Sauté the cockscomb and rooster kidneysin a pan with 1 tbsp of butter. Sprinkle with a little salt and pepper.

6. Stir half the butter into the cabbage; sauté briefly. Mound it in the center of a serving dish, reserving 2 tbsp. Arrange the veal kidneys, cockscomb and rooster kidneys around the cabbage. Add the rest of the butter to the reserved cabbage and beat vigorously. Pour this sauce around the kidneys and serve piping hot.

Stuffed Artichoke

Ingredients:
7 oz/200 g dried
   morels
4 medium artichokes
2 lemons
1 tbsp flour
2 cups/500 ml heavy
   cream
1 bunch of chervil
salt and pepper

Serves 4
Preparation time: 20 minutes
Cooking time: 30 minutes
Difficulty: ✶

1. Soak the morels in water. Peel the artichokes and shave off their bottoms so that they are flat. Place the artichokes in a bowl of water combined with the juice of one lemon and set aside.

This recipe is named after a very famous baron named Rosmadec who was known throughout Brittany, though the exact details leading to this association have become unclear with the passage of time.

To keep the artichokes from blackening, our chef suggests thoroughly rubbing them with lemon. Adding flour and lemon juice to the cooking water will also help preserve the artichoke's color. The artichokes should cook in barely boiling water.

Depending on individual taste, boil the artichokes anywhere from 15 to 25 minutes, depending on whether you prefer artichokes that offer some resistance or those with a very soft texture.

When morels are out of season, use dried morels; they are just as flavorful as fresh ones. They should soak about 24 hours before being used in cooking; this should cleanse away all the dirt and pebbles that get caught in their many folds. Also try to remember to change the soaking water several times.

When the cream in which the morels are cooked becomes thick enough to coat a wooden spoon, the morels are done and should be removed.

The artichoke's bitterness needs to be balanced by a soft but dry wine. A white Bordeaux of Rieussec will be perfect.

2. Bring a pot of water to boil. Squeeze in the juice of the second lemon. Sprinkle the flour onto the water, whisk thoroughly, and season with salt and pepper.

3. Cook the artichoke hearts in this liquid for 15 to 25 minutes.

4. In a separate pot, bring the cream to a boil.

Hearts à la Rosmadec

5. Carefully clean and rinse the morels, then stir them into the hot cream. Add salt and pepper and let simmer very gently.

6. Strain the morels from the cream sauce. Remove and discard the hairy choke from the artichoke hearts and stuff with the morels. Reduce the sauce, spoon it onto a platter, and place the stuffed artichokes in the center.

Porcini

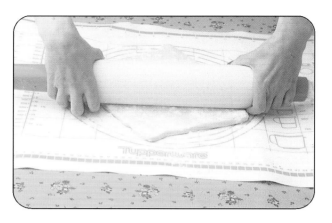

1. Prepare the puff pastry according to the basic recipe. When you are ready to proceed, Sprinkle flour on a large work surface and roll out the dough evenly.

2. Ease the pastry into a straight-sided pie pan and prick it lightly with a fork.

Ingredients:
10½ oz/300 g puff
   pastry (see basic
   recipe)
1 tbsp flour
4 shallots
¼ cup/60 g butter
2.2 lbs/1 kg large
   porcini
1 tbsp heavy cream
1 bunch of parsley
salt and pepper

Serves 4
Preparation time: 15 minutes
Cooking time: 40 minutes
Difficulty: ✻

Apart from the porcini, which are of course exquisite, another important element in the flavor of this beautiful tart is the parsley. Choose fresh parsley, preferably flat-leaf or "common" parsley. The more standard curly-leaf parsley is often used for its attractive springy leaves, but it has much less flavor than the flat-leafed variety. A little-known fact is that parsley is four times richer in vitamin C than oranges!

Our chef recommends a hot oven during the early stages of baking to guarantee a crisp crust; the heat can be reduced a few minutes into the baking time. You might also broil the top of the tart just before serving to add extra color and flavor.

When porcini mushrooms are not in season, this tart can also be prepared using ordinary mushrooms. After all, the key to this dish is not the preparation of the mushroom but the presentation of the tart itself, which at first appears to be as commonplaceas potatoes, but offers an original and pleasant surprise.

This recipe is quick and easy. Serve the tart very warm on a cool fall night.

The porcini mushrooms will go admirably well with Pauillac since they are both earthy products. Try a Château Pontet-Canet.

3. Chop the shallots and sauté them with 1 tbsp of the butter. Cut the stems from the mushrooms, setting aside the heads. Chop the stems and stir them into the shallots. Let this mixture brown.

4. Once all moisture has evaporated from the shallot mixture, salt and pepper lightly and add the cream. Let this thicken over very low heat. Remove from the heat and stir in the chopped parsley. Let cool.

Tart

5. Spread the shallot/mushroom mixture onto the pastry. Slice the porcini caps and arrange them in a spiral on top of the filling.

6. Melt the remaining butter and brush it on the sliced mushrooms. Bake at 350 °F for 30 minutes and serve hot.

Porcini and

1. Dice and blanch the bacon. Blanch the cabbage leaves in a pot of boiling salted water, then drain and cut them coarsely.

Ingredients:
8¾ oz/250 g unsliced
   bacon
½ head of cabbage
2 tbsp/30 g butter
2 carrots
7 oz/200 g porcini
2 cloves of garlic
1 sprig of thyme
1 laurel leaf
6 potatoes
salt and pepper

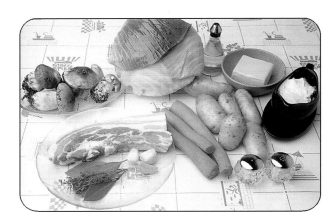

Serves 4
Preparation time: 25 minutes
Cooking time: 40 minutes
Difficulty: ✶✶

2. Sauté the bacon in a little butter. Peel and dice the carrots, then stir them in.

With this recipe our chef gives us an unusual, hearty medley of flavors. This rich appetizer is the perfect excuse to celebrate fall and the appearance of the first mushrooms of the season. It also proves that the best dishes do not necessarily entail great time and effort. Indeed, simplicity and speed are allies here and the result is beautiful.

Before blanching the cabbage, be sure to remove the tough, indigestible edges of the leaves. To maintain the color of the cabbage, the water in which it is boiled should be fairly salty. Also, the more tender the cabbage, the more easily it will fit into the mold. Cured bacon tastes better with porcini, while smoked bacon is a better choice when using ordinary mushrooms.

It may be easiest to slice the potatoes with a food processor. The thinner the slices, the easier it will be to line the mold with them.

Do not rinse the potato slices. This would remove all their starch, which is critical to their sticking together. The vegetables should be packed into the mold firmly. The more compact the ensemble, the easier it will be to unmold. You may also use a nonstick baking dish to avoid this problem.

Since the pleasure of this dish lies in the mushrooms, our wine expert suggests you open a great St. Émilion. A Château Canon, for example, one of the best wines of France, is still produced entirely in the ancient manner.

3. Slice the porcini and add them to the pan as well.

4. Add the chopped garlic, thyme, laurel, and the blanched cabbage. Lightly salt and pepper. Cover and cook over low heat for 15 minutes.

Potato Gâteau

5. Peel the potatoes and slice them very thinly. Butter a mold and line the inside with the potato slices.

6. Fill the mold with the vegetable mixture. Cover with additional potato slices. Bake in a bain-marie at 350 °F for 30 minutes, and serve very hot.

Pig's Foot

1. Wash or peel and chop the first 7 ingredients. Sauté the vegetables, then add the garlic, white wine, and the bouillon cube dissolved in 2 cups/500 ml water. Season with thyme, laurel and generous salt and pepper. Add the pig's foot, cover, and simmer for 1½ hours.

2. When cooked, remove the bones from the pig's foot. Reduce the liquid by half its original volume, then set aside. Place the boned pig's foot in a flat-bottomed bowl, cover with ¾ in/2 cm water, and refrigerate. Once it has solidified, cut out 2¼ in/6 cm rounds.

Ingredients:
1 onion; 2 cloves garlic; 2 shallots; 1 leek; 1 stalk celery; 1 tomato; 1 carrot
¾ cup/200 ml white wine
1 sprig thyme; 1 laurel leaf
1 cube beef bouillon
1 pig's foot
1 chicken breast; 1 egg white; 6½ tbsp/100 ml heavy cream
5¼ oz/150 g boiling onions
1 tbsp/15 g sugar
7 oz/200 g *trompette de la morte* mushrooms
1 pork caul
1 lb/500 g potatoes
2¾ oz/80 g lardons
1¼ cups/300 ml pork stock (see basic recipe)
5 tbsp/75 g butter
salt and pepper

Serves 3
Preparation time: 1 hour 10 minutes
Cooking time: 2 hours 10 minutes
Difficulty: ✶✶✶

Crépinettes are actually a kind of French sausage, flavored with parsley and wrapped in *crépine*, or pork caul, rather than a typical casing. Caul is a thin lace-like layer of fat that is often used not only to hold meats together, but also for decoration. This version creates much more than a sausage, but the pork and chicken fillings are indeed wrapped in *crépine* and then fried as a sausage might be. Properly prepared, they are an auspicious beginning for a meal. The truth be told, this recipe stems from the talented and renowned master chef Escoffier.

The egg white is used to consolidate the chicken mousse, and to give it more volume and shine. It can be beaten simultaneously with the chicken.

The bones should be removed from the pig's foot after cooking, while it is still warm. Keep some pressure on the pig's foot preparation as it cools, perhaps by weighting it down with a cutting board. This will help shape it. It can, of course, be prepared in advance, preferably the night before. This will save a good deal of time. Lardons and vegetables make a wonderful accompaniment.

Our wine expert suggests opening a Mâcon Lugny. This white wine from Mâcon gets along beautifully with all cuts of pork.

3. Blend the chicken meat together with the egg white and some salt and pepper. When a mousse begins to form, add the cream. Blend and refrigerate. Sauté the boiling onions a little butter and water, a pinch of salt, and the sugar. Chop the mushrooms.

4. Add the chopped mushrooms to the chicken mousse. Spread out the caul and top it with 2 tbsp of the mousse and a round of the pork. Cover with a little more mousse, then wrap in the caul to form the crépinettes. Steam the patties for about 10 minutes.

Crépinettes

5. Immediately before serving, fry the crépinettes in 1 tbsp each of butter and oil. In a separate pan, sauté the trompettes de la mort. Peel and grate the potatoes and form similar patties, slightly larger than the pork rounds. Fry the potato patties.

6. Sauté the lardons. Pour the pork stock from Step 2 on a serving platter. Set the potato patties in the stock and the crépinettes on top. Sprinkle with the mushrooms, lardons, and onions, and serve very hot.

Seared Foie Gras with

1. Caramelize the honey in a pan over very low heat. Add the onion and carrot. Sauté for a few minutes or until the honey darkens. When the honey turns an amber color, stir in the vinegar. Let this simmer for a moment, then pour in the orange juice.

Ingredients:
1 tbsp honey
1 onion, diced
1 carrot, diced
6½ tbsp/100 ml red
    wine vinegar
juice of ½ orange
1 endive
3½ tbsp/50 butter
ginger root
½ apple
½ red bell pepper
1 cube veal bouillon
7 oz/200 g duck foie
    gras
salt and pepper

Serves 3
Preparation time: 20 minutes
Cooking time: 25 minutes
Difficulty: ✶ ✶

There are countless ways to prepare foie gras; here is a somewhat less traditional one. Our chef was inspired to create this unique foie gras recipe, and he is delighted to share it with you.

When cooking with endive, there is always the risk of bitterness. Usually, though, by adding a pinch of sugar and the juice of half a lemon to the water when boiling it, you can minimize the risk and reduce the acidity.

French gastronomy has traveled around the world and come home enhanced with many exotic flavors and ingredients. Ginger is fairly new to French cuisine, but its popularity is growing. The addition of ginger to this sauce balances and unifies all the other ingredients; they become a team to enhance the foie gras. To keep the ginger from darkening as it cooks, soak it first in white wine.

Foie gras is a sign of prosperity and celebration. Little or no oil or butter is needed to sear the foie gras; it is best cooked in its own fat. This step should be quick and the pan should be very hot. Otherwise, the foie gras will dissolve in the pan.

Respect the golden wine-and-foie-gras rule: Never serve a red wine high in tannin with either endives or foie gras. Open a bottle of Savigny-lès-Beaune.

2. Clean the endive and cut into thin slices. Chop the ginger. Dissolve the bouillon cube in ¾ cup/200 ml water.

3. Peel and dice the apple; dice the red pepper.

4. Sauté the apples in a little butter, and season lightly with salt and pepper. Sauté the peppers in a separate pan. Stir the bouillon into the honey sauce.

Endive and Red Pepper

5. In a third pan, sauté the endive slices with the remaining butter and a little salt and pepper. Pour the stock sauce through a strainer. Stir in the grated ginger and let it steep.

6. Sear the foie gras in a hot nonstick pan; sprinkle with salt and pepper. Bunch the endive slices together in the middle of a serving platter. Adjust the seasoning of the sauce, if necessary, and stir in the diced apple and pepper. Pour the sauce around the endive, place the foie gras on top and serve piping hot.

Calamari

1. Clean the mushrooms, slice them, and set aside. Cut the squid into very fine strips.

Ingredients:
8¾ oz/250 g
   mushrooms
2.2 lbs/1 kg squid,
   cleaned
1¼ lbs/600 g fresh
   fettucini
5 tbsp olive oil
3 cloves garlic
1 small hot pepper
¾ cup/200 ml dry
   white wine
1 glass cognac
1¾ oz/50 g small
   shrimp
14 oz/400 g tomatoes
1 tbsp parsley
salt and pepper

Serves 4
Preparation time: 1 hour 10 minutes
Cooking time: 45 minutes
Difficulty: ✳✳

2. Boil the pasta in slightly salted water and 1 tbsp oil. Brown the squid in a pan with olive oil.

This is a great recipe for those times when you are caught offguard by unexpected guests! There is really nothing to fear. This dish, rich in protein and iodine, is easy to prepare and will please even the most demanding palate.

The squid need to soak for at least two hours in cold water. If there is not enough time to do this, you can substitute mussels or clams.

When boiling the fettucini, add a tablespoon of oil to keep the noodles from sticking to each other. And to keep the mushrooms from turning black, soak them in water with a little lemon.

In Rome and parts of northern Italy, the words "fettucine" and "tagliatelle" are interchangeable. "Tagliatelle" simply means "little cut up thing."

This festive and colorful dish brings an extra zing to a meal, and may well set everyone's heart yearning for Italy!

The sunshine emanating from this dish requires an elegant and warm wine. Our wine expert suggests a Bandol rosé.

3. As the squid begin to darken, stir in the chopped garlic and hot pepper. Add salt and pepper. Pour in the wine and cognac. Let this reduce to half its volume over high heat.

4. Sauté the sliced mushrooms in a separate pan with a little oil.

Fettucini

5. Stir the shrimp into the mushrooms, then add this mixture to the squid and combine thoroughly.

6. Peel, seed, and cube the tomatoes. Stir them into the squid and heat up for about 2 minutes. Serve warm, sprinkled with chopped parsley.

Potato and

1. Soak the prunes in warm water for an hour; pit them. Peel and grate the potatoes over a large ovenproof dish.

Ingredients:
10½ oz/300 g prunes
3¼ lbs/1.5 kg
   potatoes
5 eggs
10 tbsp/75 g flour
3 cups/750 ml warm
   milk
5 tbsp/75 g butter
salt and pepper

Serves 6
Preparation time: 1 hour 30 minutes
Cooking time: 30 minutes
Difficulty: ✶

2. Beat the eggs with the flour. Add salt and pepper and stir vigorously. Pour in the warm milk.

Here is a typical dish from the Savoy region of France. The heart of the dish is the potato, and it was often served on holidays with cold cuts or even as a main dish. Traditionally, this recipe called for dried pears and raisins in addition to prunes. In fact, you might consider replacing the prunes with raisins (soaked for ten minutes in warm water), just for the sake of variety, or remain loyal to this version and do not change a thing.

To keep the potatoes from discoloring, peel and grate them just before combining them with the liquids, rather than earlier. The flour may cause small lumps, but they can be eliminate by using a whisk.

To keep the gratin from sticking to the baking dish, butter it generously. This is a wonderful meal for vegetarians, but if you are a meat eater, try lining the baking dish with bacon. It will make unmolding a snap, and add its own special flavor.

In any case, this gratin must be removed from its baking dish. It is particularly suitable to be served with a roast, be it pork or veal.

It is our wine expert's opinion that the rustic taste of a Mondeuse de Savoie will emphasize the nobility of this regional meal.

3. Melt the butter and stir it into the milk mixture. Adjust the seasoning if necessary.

4. Pour the batter over the potatoes and combine well.

Prune Gratin

5. Add the prunes and mix gently.

6. Pour the combined ingredients in a well-greased baking dish or mold. Cover with aluminum foil and bake in a bain-marie for 1½ hours at 325 °F. Unmold the gratin immediately before serving and bring to the table very hot.

Rice

1. Heat the water and dissolve the bouillon cubes in it.

Ingredients:

6 cups/1.5 liters
 water
2 cubes chicken
 bouillon
2 onions
9 tbsp/145 g butter
1 lb/500 g long grain
 rice
1 pinch of saffron
1 oz/30 g beef
 marrow
6½ tbsp/100 ml dry
 white wine
4½ oz/120 g grated
 Parmesan cheese
salt and pepper

Serves 4
Preparation time: 15 minutes
Cooking time: 35 minutes
Difficulty: ✶

2. Peel and chop the onions. Sauté them in a pot with 1 tbsp butter for 8-10 minutes without letting them brown.

Rice is a well-traveled grain. It was first discovered and grown in China about three thousand years ago, but some claim it originated in southern India. From there, it conquered Korea, the Phillipines, Japan, Indonesia, Mesopotamia, and Greece. It inched its way toward France, where its acceptance was slow in coming. Since 1942 efforts have been made to cultivate rice in the Camargue region, where enough is grown to help meet the country's growing demand. Rice is one of the most complete grains available, and contains vitamin B, iron, and calcium.

Our chef suggests soaking the marrow in very cold water for about an hour in order to whiten it. In fact, this is a method of preservation: It can keep up to a week in the refrigerator as long as the water is changed every day.

Rice Milanese sounds like an Italian dish, but in fact, this is a regional recipe from Savoy.

This colorful and tasty rice is a delicate treat with lamb kabobs or veal chops.

Our wine expert suggests that a light wine, such as a Brouilly, will go well with this special rice.

3. Add the rice and saffron and stir over low heat for about 2 minutes.

4. Dice the marrow and stir into the rice.

Milanese

5. When the rice starts to turn translucent, pour in the wine and chicken stock. Stir and let simmer for about 20 minutes.

6. Add the remaining butter and the cheese. Toss lightly with a fork and serve warm.

Fillets of

1. Fillet the sole (see basic recipe). Skin, seed and chop the tomatoes. Peel the shallots and mince them; chop the parsley finely, then thinly slice the mushrooms.

Ingredients:
3 10½-oz/300-g sole
4 tomatoes
2 shallots
1 bunch parsley
3½ oz/100 g button
    mushrooms
1 glass white wine
¾ cup/200 ml crème
    fraîche
3½ tbsp/50 g butter
salt and pepper

Serves 4
Preparation time: 20 minutes
Cooking time: 20 minutes
Difficulty: ✳✳

2. On the stovetop, brown the shallots in a roasting pan with a little butter. Add the chopped tomato and mushroom slices and cook.

The method of cooking is important in this recipe, as it lends the finished meal its special characteristic. Our chef has scrupulously held to the method used in our grandparents' time. This fine classic dish from Lyons will be the center of attention on your table.

Our chef recommends that you make small slits along the upper side of the fillets to prevent the sole from curling up while cooking.

Place the fillets in the baking dish and cover them with greased paper, which will not stick to the fish.

As is the case with all fish fillets, you have to be careful while cooking the sole. The fillets cook very rapidly, and they quickly disintegrate when overcooked.

This charmingly old-fashioned dish can be deliciously accompanied by spinach in butter with finely chopped shallots.

If you want to surprise your friends and astonish them with the novelty of things past, serve this fish dish: They will be sure to enjoy it.

Open a bottle of Meursault Charmes (Domaine Michelot-Buisson) and discover its marvellous roasted almond aromas.

3. Place the sole fillets on top of the vegetables.

4. Season with salt and pepper. Pour in the white wine and a glass of water and cook in the oven for about 10 minutes.

Sole Glacé

5. Remove the sole fillets. Arrange them on a serving platter and keep hot. Reduce the cooking juices by half, then stir in the crème fraîche and simmer over low heat until the sauce thickens.

6. Whisk the butter into the sauce and add the chopped parsley. Adjust the seasoning if necessary. Pour the sauce over the sole fillets and serve very hot.

Trout and

1. Fillet the trouts (see basic recipe) to yield 1¼ lb/600 g fish. Remove the skin and cut the fillets into small pieces. Place them in the freezer for 15 minutes.

Ingredients:
4 lake trout
3 egg whites
¾ cup/200 ml créme fraîche
4½ lbs/2 kg clams
6½ tbsp/100 ml white wine
2 shallots
¾ cup/200 ml heavy cream
3 tbsp truffle juice
1 truffle
13 tbsp/200 g butter
salt and pepper

Serves 6
Preparation time: 35 minutes
Cooking time: 25 minutes
Difficulty: ✷✷

2. Blend the chilled trout in a food processor and add salt and pepper. Beat in the egg whites.

Our chef grew up near a lake and has always sought that "down home" feeling in his cooking. This is why he has chosen lake trout, with its delicate, pink flesh similar to the *omble chevalier* salmon. This recipe is much simpler than many trout recipes— especially the classics like "Trout Almondine" or "Trout Meuniere"—largely because the mousse can be prepared as much as a day ahead of time. The clam sauce can also be made the night before. This way, the sauce needs only to be whipped with butter and it is ready. This is a wonderful way to save time when entertaining guests or preparing a multiple course meal.

Clams are often gritty and must be washed thoroughly either by rinsing them in running water or by letting them soak. After they are steamed in white wine, be sure to pour the cooking liquid through a fine strainer to remove any sand. The wine is the foundation of the sauce and grit would ruin the whole meal.

The dumplings can be made using two soup spoons. Simply squeeze the mousse between the two spoons and the dumpling is ready. They can be tricky so do not be upset if their form is not perfect; their taste will be!

Our wine expert believes that a Vouvray has an affinity for truffles, not to mention a lot of class. Open a bottle of dry Vouvray (Domaine G.-Huet).

3. Add the créme fraîche. Beat until the mousse is very smooth and homogenous.

4. In a large pot, steam the clams with the wine and chopped shallots. Drain well, reserving all the cooking juices. Pour the liquid through a strainer, then return to the heat and reduce its volume by half.

Truffle Dumplings

5. Bring a pot of slightly salted water to a boil. With two wet spoons, form dumplings of trout mousse and poach them in water that is just boiling. When done, drain them and set aside.

6. Add the cream and truffle juice to the reduced wine. Let the sauce thicken over low heat. Strain again, adjust the seasoning, stir in the chopped truffle and let it steep in the sauce. Whisk in the butter and pour over the dumplings. Serve with the clams, removed from their shell.

Sausage with

1. Let the sausage simmer in water for 25 minutes.

Ingredients:
- 1 1¾-lb/800-g
  sausage in casing
- 2 onions
- 3 carrots
- 4 leeks
- 1 cube veal bouillon
- ¾ cup/200 ml water
- 1 bottle red wine
- 1 bouquet garni
- whole cloves
- 5 juniper berries
- 1 tbsp mustard seeds
- 1 tbsp butter
- ½ tsp potato starch
- 2 tbsp port
- salt and pepper

Serves 6
Preparation time: 15 minutes
Cooking time: 45 minutes
Difficulty: *

Warm sausage served with white beans, potatoes and lentils is a traditional dish of the Lyon region. Our recipe updates this tradition. Our chef prefers to boil the sausage in unsalted water; in fact, he recommends soaking the sausage beforehand to remove some of the salt already in the meat. To keep the sausage from bursting when cooking, aim for a simmer rather than a rolling boil. Obviously, you should buy the freshest possible sausage, and avoid smoked sausages. A sausage with light meat has generally been made with better-quality meat, such as ham and shoulder, whereas darker sausages are often made with fattier, cheaper cuts of pork and byproducts.

Our chef has also chosen another traditional combination, red wine and leeks. Choose a good red wine, rich in tannin such as a Côtes-du-Rhône. Let the wine cook slowly; this will allow it to surrender its natural acidity.

Do not use too much potato starch. Its purpose is merely to help the sauce thicken. The sausage should barely touch the sauce. One very interesting alternative is a sausage—as used here—that contains pistachios and truffles.

Our wine expert suggests the wild charm of a red St. Joseph.

2. Peel and chop the onion; slice the carrot and 1 leek.

3. Dissolve the bouillon cube in the water. Pour the red wine in a pot and add the onions, carrot, leek, bouquet garni, and cloves.

4. Stir in the juniper berries and mustard seeds. Add salt and pepper. Let this reduce by half its original volume.

Red Wine and Leeks

5. Clean the remaing leeks and cut them into thin slices. Let them sweat in a large pan with the butter.

6. Adjust the seasoning of the sauce; combine the potato starch with the port and add them to it. Slice the sausage and serve with the leeks and sauce.

Eel Stew

1. Skin and gut the eel and cut it into 1½ in/3 cm chunks.

Ingredients:

2.2 lbs/1 kg eel
6½ tbsp/100 g butter
3½ oz/100 g white bread
5¼ oz/150 g mushrooms
5¼ oz/150 g smoked bacon
4 cups/1 liter red wine
1 cube chicken bouillon
5¼ oz/150 g boiling onions
chives
parsley
salt and pepper

Serves 4
Preparation time: 30 minutes
Cooking time: 30 minutes
Difficulty: ✶

2. Sauté the eel in a pan with 2 tbsp butter over high heat. Add salt and pepper.

This regional recipe originates in the Loire Valley and along the Rhône river. In the Basque region, in Hendaye, a local brandy is often added. This general type of stew comes in myriad forms. It might be made with red or white wine, and with any of a variety of freshwater fish such as eel, carp, trout, pike, shad, or herring. Eel is a fairly fatty fish but it is rich in vitamins A and B2 and calcium. Preparing eel is often a slow task and gutting it takes time. Usually, however, you can have the fish monger do this for you. If eel is not available, substitute conger eel or monkfish.

This dish should be served warm and is excellent with pasta. Conveniently, it takes well to being reheated.

Because eel has a very distinct flavor, one is often better off serving it only to guests who have had it before. Eel has too strong a taste to serve to an unwitting guest.

It is difficult to find a wine to match the eel's flavor. However, our wine expert suggests a wine from a totally different region. Try a Pineau d'Aunis or a Muscadet sur lie.

3. Cut the white bread into small cubes. Cube the mushrooms and dice the bacon.

4. Bring the red wine to a boil, let simmer for 5 minutes, then pour it over the eel. Dissolve the bouillon cube in a glass of water and stir this into the eel and wine. Add salt and pepper and cook over low heat for 15 minutes.

with Red Wine

5. Sauté the mushrooms, bacon, and bread in three separate pans, each with a little butter. Poach the onions in lightly salted water.

6. When the eel is done, remove it and arrange on a serving platter. Strain the sauce, return it to the heat, and let it reduce to half its original volume. Whisk in the remaining butter and adjust the seasoning. Garnish with parsley and chives, if desired, and serve warm.

Pot-au-Feu with

1. Clean or peel and trim all the small, young vegetables. Clean and quarter the leek.

Ingredients:
1 leek
3 carrots
3 stalks of celery, halved
4 turnips
3½ oz/100 g butter or fava beans
4 boiling onions
4 cabbage leaves
2 lamb's brains
⅓ cup/80 ml vinegar
2 tbsp tapioca
13 tbsp/200 g butter
1 bunch chives
5¼ oz/150 g snails
4 tbsp/30 g flour
salt and pepper

Serves 4
Preparation time: 30 minutes
Cooking time: 35 minutes
Difficulty: ✶

2. Bring 6 cups/1.5 liters of lightly salted water to a boil. Poach the leek, carrots, celery, turnips, beans and boiling onions. The vegetables should remain slightly crisp. Reserve the cooking liquid.

A snail hides in its shell like a monk hides under his cowl. No doubt this is what our French ancestors had in mind when they nicknamed the snail *cagoule*, which is a hat that covers the entire head. The name has stuck, with some modifications, and snails are often referred to in France as *cagouilles*.

Snails are appreciated for their fine, fruity flavor and the delicate consistency of their flesh. If you are unable to gather them yourself, try to locate some at the market. In summer as in winter, snails are generally not difficult to find, though they will be thinner in the winter months; or you may use canned snails. If snails prove too difficult to find or are not your cup of tea, try preparing this dish with beef.

This regional recipe is not difficult to prepare but it is time-consuming, largely because of the time involved in peeling all the vegetables. Select young, fresh "baby" vegetables, if at all possible. This dish should be served warm, but can also be eaten as a leftover.

Our wine expert suggests a Chablis Fourchaumes. Archeological digs have revealed that the Chablis region is filled with fossilized snail and oyster shells. Hence, if for no other reason, Chablis is an obvious choice.

3. Choose 4 large, whole leaves of cabbage. Clean well and set aside. Bring 3 pots of slightly salted water to boil.

4. Blanch the cabbage leaves in one pot. Poach the brains with a little vinegar in another, and cook the tapioca in the third.

Snails and Cabbage

5. Sauté the snails in a little butter. Add salt and pepper and stir in the chives. Coat the brains in flour and sauté them separately.

6. To prepare the sauce, considerably reduce the cooking water from Step 2. Stir in the tapioca, then whisk in the remaining butter. Arrange the vegetables on a serving dish. Wrap the brains in cabbage leaves and place them on the vegetables, and sprinkle the snails on top. Serve warm with the sauce.

Cannellini

1. Chop the onion and brown in a pot with 1 tbsp butter.

Ingredients:
3½ oz/100 g onion
3½ tbsp/50 g butter
3½ oz/100 g carrot
3 tomatoes
1 bouquet garni
5¼ oz/150 g bacon
1 boiling onion
5 whole cloves
1 lb/500 g white
   kidney beans, pre-
   soaked
3 cloves garlic
salt and pepper

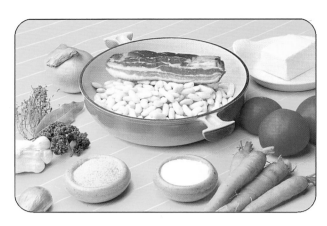

Serves 4
Preparation time: 15 minutes
Cooking time: 2 hours
Difficulty: ✶

Cannellini and white kidney beans are two names for the same legume. Often considered a traditional country dish, these beans still have an interesting history. Originating in the Americas, they were supposedly brought to France in the sixteenth century by Pope Clement VII as a wedding gift for his niece, Catherine de Medicis. The trend nowadays is to serve beans with fish, though traditionally they have always been served with lamb. It is said that beans like their feet in the water and their head in the sun. They are usually harvested between July and October. Fresh beans can be frozen and beans that have been frozen have a far better taste and texture than reconstituted dried ones.

This regional recipe is easy to prepare, but one must think ahead. The beans should be soaked in water ovenight and carefully supervised as they cook. To keep them from becoming tough, wait until the end of the preparation to add salt. These beans can also be eaten cold, after being rinsed with a little vinaigrette.

Our wine expert suggests a red Bordeaux, a Bourgueil, to add a perfect rustic touch.

2. Peel and chop the carrots into small dice. Brown them with the onion.

3. Peel, seed, and quarter the tomatoes. Stir them into the onions and carrots and sauté a few minutes.

4. Add the bouquet garni, the bacon, and the boiling onion, studded with the whole cloves. Let this mixture simmer very lightly, stirring occasionally.

Beans

5. Drain the kidney beans well after soaking and add to the vegetable preparation. Add the garlic and let it steep.

6. Pour some water over the beans and simmer for about 1 hour. After about 55 minutes, season with salt and pepper. Serve hot.

Artichokes with

1. Remove the leaves from the artichokes and trim any uneven edges with a knife. Do not cut off the stem. Soak them in water along with the lemon juice.

Ingredients:
2¾ lbs/1.3 kg
 artichokes
juice of 2 lemons
3½ tbsp/50 g butter
7 oz/200 g boiling
 onions
1 tbsp sugar
4 slices smoked
 bacon
1 tbsp flour
1 clove garlic
1/2 bottle Gamay de
 Touraine
1 bunch of parsley
salt and pepper

Serves 5
Preparation time: 25 minutes
Cooking time: 25 minutes
Difficulty: ✶

2. Drain the artichoke hearts and cut them from top to bottom, making four slices. Briefly blanch the boiling onions.

Artichokes were born in Sicily. In France they were originally only used for medicinal purposes. At the beginning of the eighteenth century, Lemery's *Traité des aliments* claimed that "Artichokes are appropriate at any time for elderly people with a phlegmatic and melancholic temperament." But this is not all! Apparently, the artichoke was considered an aphrodisiac, and therefore proscribed for women. Catherine de Medicis, with her commanding personality, was very fond of artichokes and encouraged their cultivation in France. We owe her our gratitude.

Now it is our chef's turn to take advantage of the virtues of the artichoke. Fresh artichokes are firm and heavy, with crisp, tight leaves. You can judge their freshness by their leaves: If the tops are turning black, they are old.

Our chef suggests lightly browning the artichoke hearts on each side and chopping the garlic before the artichokes cook. Also, she warns, add no more than 1 tbsp of flour to the sauce, or it will become too thick. This dish should be served warm, right after cooking, for it does not keep. This is a rich appetizer, easy to prepare, and will come in handy as an accompaniment for fish.

The pleasantly fruity taste of a Gamay de Touraine will be just the thing to counteract the slight bitterness of the artichoke.

3. Brown the artichoke slices in a pan with a little butter and set them aside. Sauté the boiling onions in butter and sprinkle them with a spoonful of sugar.

4. Chop the bacon and stir it into the onions. Sauté briefly and set aside.

Red Gamay

5. Sprinkle the flour over the juice left in the pan and let the flour absorb the cooking juices.

6. Pour in the wine and bring to a light boil. Add the artichoke hearts, onions and bacon, and simmer over low heat for 5-6 minutes. Stir in the garlic and adjust the seasoning. Sprinkle with parsley and serve.

Langoustine and

1. Slice the carrot and onion. Heat a pot of water and add the carrot, onion, bouquet garni, and lemon juice. When it begins to boil, introduce the langoustines and poach them for 10 minutes.

Ingredients:
1 carrot
1 onion
1 bouquet garni
juice of 1 lemon
2.2 lbs/1 kg
   langoustines
5¼ oz/150 g fresh
   pasta
6½ tbsp/100 ml
   créme fraîche
3 tbsp tarragon
6 eggs
3½ tbsp/50 g butter
salt and pepper

Serves 6
Preparation time: 15 minutes
Cooking time: 50 minutes
Difficulty: ✶

2. Drain the langoustines. Remove the meat from the shell and pour the cooking liquid through a strainer to remove any grit. Reheat this broth and cook the pasta in it.

For the pasta in this recipe, our chef suggests fettucini, since it will be easy to cut when serving the soufflé. Fettucine is an Italian pasta, a specialty of Emilia-Romagna, in the region near Bologne. Legend has it that a nobleman who was terribly in love with Lucrecia Borgia's hair invented fettucini so that he could pretend to have the unattainable on his plate. To keep the pasta from sticking to itself, add a spoonful of oil to the water in which it is cooked.

Lobster or crayfish can be substituted for the langoustines. For that matter, this soufflé is equally delicious made with the fillet of any white fish.

This is a very simple but delicate dish to prepare. Serve it as soon as it is removed from the oven, for a soufflé will fall faster than it rose. Do not keep the soufflé waiting, for it cannot be reheated.

Our wine expert suggests that a white Bandol from the south of France will be a good choice to complement the Italian influences of this dish.

3. Once the pasta is al dente, drain it and place in a bowl. Add the créme fraîche and tarragon and stir to combine.

4. Separate the eggs. Stir the yolks into the pasta; season with salt and pepper.

Pasta Soufflé

5. Whip the egg whites until stiff and gently fold them into the pasta mixture.

6. In a buttered soufflé dish, layer the pasta with the langoustine meat, beginning with pasta. Do not exceed the height of the baking dish. Bake the soufflé for 30 minutes at 400 °F, and serve immediately.

Tongue

1. Blanch the tongue in a pot of slightly salted boiling water for about 20 minutes.

Ingredients:
½ veal tongue
3 cloves of garlic
3 onions
2 carrots
6½ tbsp/100 g butter
1 bouquet garni
5¼ oz/150 g lentils
salt and pepper

Serves 4
Preparation time: 15 minutes
Cooking time: 55 minutes
Difficulty: ✶

2. Peel and slice the garlic, onions, and carrots.

For hundreds of years, lentils have been regarded as poor people's fare. This may explain their relative unpopularity today. It is, however, an injustice and a waste. Not only are lentils delicious and versatile, they are also extremely nutritious—rich in protein, glucose, calcium, phosphorus, iron, and vitamin B. One suggestion, which holds for any dried vegetable: Do not salt the water until the vegetable is almost finished cooking. The salt will cause the vegetable to toughen if it is added too soon.

This wonderful stew should be served very hot; it can also be made with beef or pork if you prefer a meatier dish. It is just as good when warmed up and will keep for two to three days in the refrigerator.

Our wine expert insists that lentils and Cahors seek each other out and are a terrific pair when united. Try opening a bottle from the Domaine de Quattre.

3. Lightly sauté the onions and carrots in butter. Add the bouquet garni.

4. Stir the lentils into the vegetables, and season with salt and pepper.

Stew

5. Peel the tongue and cut it into bite-size pieces. Add the cubed tongue to the lentils, along with the garlic, and combine thoroughly.

6. Add enough water to cover all the ingredients. Lightly salt and pepper, then cover and simmer for 30 minutes. Serve the stew hot.

Liver Roulades

1. Trim the liver and chop the trimmings, which should be about 1½ oz/50 g. Peel and chop the onions. Poach the endives in a saucepan of salted water with 1 lemon and its juice.

2. Using a food processor, chop the smoked bacon and the liver trimmings.

3. Add the bread crumbs to this stuffing mixture and season with a little pepper, nutmeg and cayenne pepper.

Ingredients:
4 slices calf liver
2 onions
4 endives
2 lemons
4 slices smoked bacon
6½ tbsp/100 g dried bread crumbs
nutmeg
cayenne pepper
parsley
2 egg yolks
flour to coat
5 tbsp/75 g butter
3 tbsp oil
1 glass red wine
salt and pepper

Serves 4
Preparation time: 30 minutes
Cooking time: 20 minutes
Difficulty: ✶✶

Roulades are most often made using thin slices of veal. Here, our chef has decided to make them doubly as tender by using calf's liver. She suggest using liver of the very highest quality, of course.

Endives are a low-fat vegetable, ideal for slimming diets. But the fact that they are very low in calories does not stop them from being rich in potassium. Select white endives with firm, crisp leaves that are pale yellow at the ends. Adding lemon juice to the water in which they are cooked will prevent discoloration.

After draining the endives, you can enhance this dish further by cutting them in two and placing a spoonful of filling reserved for this purpose on each half. Sprinkle bread crumbs over each endive half, top with a dollop of butter, and fry until golden brown over high heat for 10 minutes.

Liver Roulades with Endives give you the opportunity to prepare a magnificent dish with calf liver, a food which is very good for children. They provide an exquisite dish for small meals, giving them all the allure of a banquet.

The slightly bitter endives and the calf liver will do well with the fruitiness of a Ladoix, which will balance out this dish perfectly.

4. Add the chopped onion and parsley and the juice of the second lemon; blend everything thoroughly. Add the egg yolks and blend again for several seconds.

with Endive

5. Coat 1 side of each slice of liver with the above mixture. Roll up the liver and fasten with toothpicks. Season with salt and pepper, then coat the rolls in flour. Brown the poached endives in a pan with a little butter.

6. Fry the roulades in a little butter and oil over low heat. Pour off the fat, add the red wine and reduce by half. Little salt and pepper, stir in a bit of butter and bring to a boil. Serve the rouladen very hot with the endives crumbed as described in the introduction and the sauce as accompaniment.

Court-Bouillon (With Lobster)

Ingredients:
1 lobster
For the bouillon:
2 carrots
1 leek
1 celery stalk
1 onion
1 shallot
whole cloves
2 cloves of garlic
1 bouquet garni
tarragon
rosemary
6½ tbsp/100 ml white wine
coarse salt and
   peppercorns

Preparation time: 15 minutes
Cooking time: 15 minutes
Difficulty: ✻

1. Peel and carefully clean all the vegetables. Stud the shallot with cloves; slice the other vegetables finely. Add them all to a large pot filled with water. Add the bouquet garni, tarragon and a sprig of rosemary.

2. Pour in the white wine and bring to a boil. Season with coarse salt and pepper and allow to simmer for 10 minutes, then strain and cool.

Court-bouillon is a spiced and aromatic stock most often used in the cooking of fish or crustaceans, but it can also be used to prepare light meats or white organ meats.

The basic preparation involves adding carrots, quartered onions (one or two of which can be studded with a few whole cloves), a bouquet garni and coarse salt to a pot of water. The court-bouillon may also be prepared with white wine, the juice of two lemons or even white vinegar, which may be added at the end of the cooking process. After simmering to extract the flavors of the ingredients, the court-bouillon should be strained, cooled, and then reheated as a broth for the preparation of the fish, lobster, or other main ingredient.

3. For a lobster: Immerse the crustacean in the court-bouillon before or after straining, according to personal preference, and simmer for 15 minutes. Remove and drain. The lobster is ready to eat.

Crêpe Batter

Ingredients:
- 2 generous cups/250 g flour
- 2 tbsp butter
- a pinch of salt
- 6 eggs
- 6½ tbsp/100 g superfine sugar
- 3 cups/750 ml milk
- zest of 1 lime
- 3½ tbsp/50 ml aged rum

Preparation time: 15 minutes
Resting time: 1 hour
Difficulty: ✷✷

1. Sift the flour into a large bowl. Melt the butter, cool slightly, and stir it in with a pinch of salt. Break in the eggs, then add the sugar.

Crêpes are deceptively simple. While they require nothing particularly difficult or fancy, some care is needed in preparing perfect crêpes.

Cook them a heavy-bottomed pan so that they do not stick.

Let the batter rest for about an hour before actually making the crêpes; in fact, it will keep for one or two days in the refrigerator.

Crêpes are incredibly versatile, and can be used as the basis for a variety of recipes. If you want to prepare a dish based on savory crêpes, omit the lime zest and sugar from this recipe.

Crêpes are suitable for serving at any time of day. Whatever way you choose to prepare them, they will always be greeted with enthusiasm.

2. Stir these ingredients until the batter is smooth and free of lumps. Pour in the milk, stirring vigorously. Add the lime zest and the rum. Mix well with a whisk. Let the batter rest at least 1 hour before making the crêpes.

3. Lightly butter a frying pan, but only for the first few crêpes. Make the crêpes as thin as possible.

Beurre Blanc (Beurre Nantais)

1. Peel the shallots and chop them finely. Brown them in a saucepan in a little butter. Pour in the vinegar and white wine, then reduce over low heat.

Ingredients:
3 shallots
3½ tbsp/50 ml vinegar
6½ tbsp/100 ml white wine
3 tbsp crème fraîche
1 cup/250 g butter
salt

Preparation time: 10 minutes
Cooking time: 10 minutes
Difficulty ✶✶

2. When the vinegar and wine have evaporated, add the crème fraiche. Stir and bring briefly to a boil.

The simplest dishes can become elegant meals when they are accompanied by tasty sauces. In the case of this *beurre nantais*, which is a smooth and exquisite sauce that accompanies many dishes in the Angevin region and the area around Nantes, good quality butter will give the sauce a particularly subtle flavor. *Beurre nantais*, which is usually flavored with aromatic herbs such as fennel, parsley, chives or tarragon, lends a delicate savor to fish dishes, one recognised and appreciated by fine gourmets.

If you strain out the shallots, and add lemon juice and a little water while incorporating the butter, you will obtain a classic *beurre blanc*. *Beurre blanc* is more neutral than *beurre nantais*, which makes it an ideal accompaniment for dishes that require little seasoning.

In both cases, be sure that the butter is well-chilled when whisking it into the sauce or it will not thicken it properly. Whisk continuously to incorporate enough air to give your butter sauce a thick, yet light consistency.

3. Cut the very cold butter into pieces, then add it gradually to the sauce while whisking constantly. Salt the sauce lightly. Strain it through a sieve to remove the shallots, if desired.

Filleting Fish

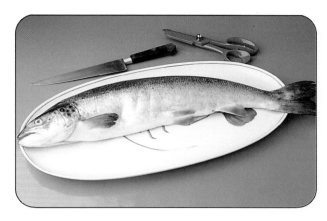

Ingredients:
1 whole fish
Knife

Preparation time: 10 minutes
Difficulty ✶✶

1. Remove the fins. Open the fish along its back and run the knife down the backbone. Cut the fillet at the top, removing it from the head. Lift the whole fillet by running the knife along the side bones.

Removing fillets from a fish is a delicate operation.
Before you begin, make sure that your tools are appropriate to the task. The knife should be long, sharp, and flexible in order to glide along the bone.
The technique is the same for all fish, with the exception of particularly thin fish, such as sole, or particularly thick ones, such as tuna.
This is a precise operation that demands care. Follow the directions scrupulously to remove the bones without damaging the fillets.

2. Turn the fish over and repeat.

3. Remove the skin by carefully sliding the knife between the skin and the flesh.

Filleting Sole

1. Remove the black skin from the sole. Turn it over and remove the white skin. Trim the fish with a pair of kitchen scissors.

Ingredients:
1 sole or other flatfish
Knife
Scissors

Preparation time: 20 minutes
Difficulty: ✭✭

2. Cut open the sole along the backbone using a pointed knife with a flexible blade. Slide the knife under the fillet, starting near the head and pressing against the backbone. Repeat with the second fillet on the first side. Trim the fillets to neaten their edges.

Smaller flatfish like sole must be skinned before they can be filleted. You may wish to ask for this to be done when you purchase the fish. Use a knife with a long, pointed blade to fillet fish to ensure that the meat will not be torn in the process.

Unlike thicker fish, flatfish yield four fillets: one above and below the backbone on each side. To begin, carefully insert the knife between the upper end of the fillet (just at the base of the head) and the ventral bones. Lift the fillet slightly and separate it from the bone a little at a time while holding the fillet with your thumb. Once the fillet is detached near the head, it is quite easily separated from the bones along the entire length of the fish by sliding the knife along the backbone. Then simply cut the fillet from the tail and trim the edges.

Follow the same procedure for the second fillet. Then turn the fish over and remove the other two fillets. The bones and trimmings can, of course, be used to make a fish stock (see basic recipe).

3. Turn over the sole and again cut along the central backbone. Repeat the procedure to detach the other 2 fillets. Beat the fillets to flatten them and break the nerves, then soak for 20 minutes in cold water. The sole fillets are now ready to use.

Madeira Sauce

Ingredients:
2 shallots
3½ tbsp/50 g butter
⅔ cup/150 ml Madeira
2 cups/500 ml meat stock
   (see basic recipe)
salt and pepper

Preparation time: 5 minutes
Cooking time: 15 minutes
Difficulty ✳

1. Peel and finely mince the shallots. Sauté until golden brown in 1 tbsp of the butter. Stir in the Madeira and simmer until reduced by half.

This delicately flavored sauce will enhance any meat dish with a subtle flavor. Guests will appreciate your special efforts as they enjoy this original and flavorful sauce.
Madeira sauce is easily prepared, yet it will give you a reputation worthy of a great cordon bleu chef. Its secret lies in the successful combination of spices, meat, and wine.
Truly a bouquet of aromas for the palate, this succulent sauce is sure to become a fixture of your cuisine.

2. Pour in the meat stock and simmer slowly for another 15 minutes. Strain the sauce through a fine sieve.

3. Reheat the sauce for a few minutes. Just before serving, remove from the heat and swirl or whisk in the remaining butter in small pieces.

Puff Pastry

Ingredients:
2½ lbs/1.3 kg cake flour
4 generous cups/1 kg
   butter
2 tbsp/35 g salt
2 cups/500 ml ice-cold
   water
flour for the work surface

1. Blend 2½ cups/300 g flour into all but 6½ tbsp/100 g of the butter and refrigerate. Mound the remaining flour, make a well in its center and place the salt, reserved butter, and a little ice-cold water in it. Begin to knead with the fingertips, adding just enough water to yield a pliable paste. Refrigerate for 30 minutes.

Preparation time: 1 hour 30 minutes
Cooking time: 20 minutes
Chilling time: 2 hours
Difficulty ✶ ✶ ✶

The ideal surface for making puff pastry is a marble countertop or cutting board, especially in the summer months when the pastry must be kept as cold as possible.

Though puff pastry can be temperamental and requires a certain touch, if you follow these directions closely, your pastry is sure to be a success.

The dough must be made quickly and kneaded firmly, yet with a light touch to retain the air pockets that give puff pastry its characteristic layers. Keep the pastry as cold as possible, and work it with your fingertips.

When all the flour has been incorporated, form the dough into a ball and make a few cuts in it to allow air to circulate. Refrigerate in between steps.

When you have created your masterpiece, brush the outer layer of pastry with beaten egg before baking to give it a golden sheen.

2. Working quickly, roll the dough into a wide rectangle. Place the butter and flour mixture in its center. Fold the pastry over the butter mixture. Carefully, again roll out the pastry into a long rectangular strip. Fold in thirds with the ends overlapping in the middle. This is 1"turn" of the dough. Repeat the process 2 more times.

3. Refrigerate the dough for 1 hour. Remove it and perform 4 more turns. Refrigerate again, and finish with 6 additional turns. The pastry is now ready to be used in any way you like.

Duck or Pigeon Stock

Ingredients:
1 duck or 3 pigeons
2 carrots
2 onions
1 celery stalk
2 cloves of garlic
1 bouquet garni
whole cloves
2 tomatoes
1 cube chicken bouillon
6½ tbsp/100 ml white wine
  (for duck)
6½ tbsp/100 ml red wine
  (for pigeon)
3½ tbsp/50 ml oil
salt and pepper

Preparation time: 20 minutes
Cooking time: 40 minutes
Difficulty ✶

1. Singe, clean and bone the fowl, reserving the meat for another recipe. Clean, pare, and dice the carrots, onions, celery and garlic. In a heavy pot, sear the duck carcass or the pigeon bones in hot oil until they are well-browned.

Traditionally duck or pigeon stock was prepared after browning the fowl. Then the *mirepoix*—a mixture of diced vegetables including onions and carrots and often others, and browned in butter—was added for flavor. The fat was poured off, and the pan deglazed with water. Herbs, cloves, salt, and pepper were added, and the stock was left to slowly simmer. Today it is more often the case that only selected pieces of the bird, notably the breast, are called for in recipes. This means that you need to ask your butcher for the trimmings, carcass and bones from the fowl to use in preparing the stock.

To extract the maximum flavor, crush the bones and carcass and brown them well in very hot oil along with the trimmings.

2. When the bones are quite brown, add the mirepoix, bouquet garni and cloves. Season with salt and pepper and add the peeled, seeded and diced tomatoes. Pour in the wine and continue cooking until the vegetables begin to take on color and soften.

3. Dissolve the bouillon cube in 4 cups/1 liter water and pour it over the ingredients in the pot. Simmer for 40 minutes. Strain this stock through a fine sieve. The stock is now ready to use.

Fish Stock

Ingredients:
2 carrots
1 leek
2 cloves of garlic
2 onions
whole cloves
3½ tbsp/50 ml oil
bones from 2 fish
1 bouquet garni
¾ cup/200 ml white wine
salt and pepper

Preparation time: 10 minutes
Cooking time: 30 minutes
Difficulty ✶

1. Clean, peel and chop the carrots, leek, garlic and one onion. Stud the whole onion with cloves. Brown the vegetables in a saucepan with a little oil. Add the cleaned bones, then the whole onion and bouquet garni, and cook tightly covered over low heat.

This fish stock is a seasoned, concentrated court-bouillon made using fish bones and trimmings. It will enable you to flavor and enhance other stocks and sauces, which are important for giving the final touch to many fish recipes.

If strained through a fine sieve and stored in a tightly sealed container, this stock will keep for several days in the refrigerator.

One of the least demanding aspects of this recipe is that it can be made from the bones of any kind of fish.

If the stock is allowed to reduce even further than instructed here, you will obtain a fairly thick liquid, a demi-glace, which is closer to a glaze and can be served in place of a sauce. Finally, be sure to clean the fish heads and bones very thoroughly before using them to create the stock.

2. Add the white wine and enough water to cover the contents of the pan. Season with salt and pepper and let simmer for 30 minutes or so over low heat.

3. Once the stock is done, strain it through a fine sieve. It is now ready to be used.

Langoustine Consommé

1. Peel and chop the onion and carrots; stud the shallot with the cloves. Break the heads off the langoustines and sauté them in very hot oil. Add the chopped vegetables and bouquet garni. Let brown.

Ingredients:
1 onion
2 carrots
1 shallot
whole cloves
1 lb/500 g langoustine heads
6½ tbsp/100 ml olive oil
1 bouquet garni
1 tbsp tomato paste
⅔ cup/150 ml white wine
salt and pepper

Preparation time: 25 minutes
Cooking time: 1 hour
Difficulty ✶✶

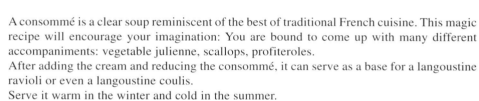

A consommé is a clear soup reminiscent of the best of traditional French cuisine. This magic recipe will encourage your imagination: You are bound to come up with many different accompaniments: vegetable julienne, scallops, profiteroles.

After adding the cream and reducing the consommé, it can serve as a base for a langoustine ravioli or even a langoustine coulis.

Serve it warm in the winter and cold in the summer.

Very simple to prepare, a consommé is always a welcome element of a meal and will be enthusiastically received by anyone.

2. Stir in the tomato paste and the shallot; add salt and pepper. Pour in the white wine and enough water to just cover the ingredients.

3. Simmer the ingredients for 1 hour, then pour through a strainer. The consommé can be served as a soup, or used as a stock.

Short Pastry

Ingredients:
2 generous cups/250 g
  flour
1 egg
10 tbsp/150 g butter
4 tsp/20 g sugar
1 pinch of salt
water

1. Sift the flour onto a smooth work surface in a mound. Make a well in the center and break the egg into it. Mix these 2 ingredients.

Preparation time: 10 minutes
Difficulty ✲

Short pastry is the most common pastry for either savory or sweet tarts and pies. This pastry is very simple to prepare.

In French there are two terms for short pastry: it is called *pâte brisée* when it is used for a pie or tart. When it is used for a turnover or dumpling, it is called *pâtè à foncer*, and no sugar is added in the basic preparation.

For savory recipes, use oil instead of butter, and add less water to the dough. Use just enough water so that the dough is neither too moist nor too dry.

Short pastry can be prepared the day before it will be used. Wrap it in a dishtowel and keep it in the refrigerator. Remove the pastry 15 minutes before rolling it out.

Short pastry is very easy to use and is not fragile, so experiment to your heart's content!

2. Add the butter, sugar, and salt. Begin kneading the dough and add a little water at a time until it just forms a smooth paste.

3. When the pastry is smooth and well-kneaded, flatten it with the palm of your hand. Let it sit 30–40 minutes before using.

Fish Mousse

1. Cut the chilled fish fillet(s) into chunks and purée.

Ingredients:
1 lb/500 g fish fillet
3 egg whites
¾ cup/200 ml heavy cream
salt and pepper

Preparation time: 20 minutes
Cooking time: 30 minutes
Difficulty ✲ ✲

2. Add the egg whites to the fish, season with salt and pepper, and blend thoroughly.

Hot or cold, as a main dish or accompaniment, this is a recipe that has more than one trick up its sleeve. This quick and easy mousse can be prepared with all sorts of fish, both freshwater and saltwater.

Our chef has these words of advice: The fish used to make the mousse and the mold into which it will be turned should always be well-chilled. Brush the mold with melted butter to avoid any trouble when turning out the mousse onto a serving platter.

Served hot, this mousse forms an excellent accompaniment to shrimps, mussels, oysters, prawns, mushrooms... The options are endless. Served as a cold dish with salad (tomatoes, avocados, hard-boiled eggs, anchovies...), our chef suggests accompanying it with a mayonnaise sauce flavored with tomato concentrate and a touch of cognac.

This recipe lends itself to experimentation and can be varied almost infinitely with the addition of various combinations of herbs and fish. Enjoy!

3. Add the well-chilled crème fraiche and blend the mixture once more until it is very smooth. Use the fish mousse following our suggestions, or if you wish, bake it in a terrine and serve it simply accompanied by melted butter.

Pasta Dough

Ingredients:
⅔ cup/300 g flour
3 eggs
2 tbsp/30 g butter, softened
salt

1. Sift the flour onto a generous work surface, making a mound. Make a well in the center and break the eggs inside it. Salt lightly.

Preparation time: 10 minutes
Resting time: 2 hours
Difficulty ✶

Not only is pasta no longer a specialty of Italians, with a recipe like this one, it will soon become a specialty of your own.

Excellent pasta consists essentially of flour, eggs and butter. The egg white gives the pasta its firmness, and the yolk lends its rich color.

It is important that the pasta dough be homogeneous; to obtain this consistency, it should be kneaded very thoroughly. It should also have time to rest. When this is done, separate the dough into four parts and roll out each into thin strips. Avoid tearing the pasta, for it is difficult to mend.

2. Add the softened butter.

3. Knead the pasta until it no longer sticks to the board. Form the dough into a ball. Slash the surface of the ball and refrigerate for 2 hours before proceeding to roll out the dough and form any type of noodles desired.

Pork Stock

Ingredients:
10½ oz/300 g pork
   trimmings and bones
3½ tbsp/50 ml oil
2 carrots
2 onions
1 stalk of celery
1 bouquet garni
whole cloves
1 tomato
2 cloves of garlic
6½ tbsp/100 ml white wine
1 cube chicken bouillon
salt and pepper

Preparation time: 10 minutes
Cooking time: 40 minutes
Difficulty ✳

1. Chop the trimmings and crush any bones, then sear them in a heavy pan with the oil. Clean, peel and coarsely chop the vegetables. When the trimmings are well browned, add the vegetables, bouquet garni, and cloves. Stir and continue cooking until the vegetables color up and begin to soften.

For a cook, meat stock is what corresponds to a foundation for everything else. This pork stock is very flavorful and takes less time to make than more traditional preparations. Moreover, it is light and adds a delicious aroma to any dish it accompanies.

Traditionally, when entire joints of meat were roasted, the fat was poured off, the pan was deglazed with water, and chopped vegetables were added. Stock prepared in this manner cooked for only about 15 minutes.

Today cooking large roasts is less common, and modern recipes call for boned and trimmed meats. So although modern practice turns to these bones and trimmings to flavor the stock, the principle remains the same.

2. Cut the tomato into pieces and add it to the pan along with the garlic. Pour in the wine and dissolve the bouillon cube in 4 cups/1 liter water.

3. Add the bouillon to the broth, season with salt and pepper, and allow to simmer for 30 to 40 minutes, then strain. The stock is ready to use.

Glossary

BAIN-MARIE: A gentle method of heating used to either cook food or keep cooked food warm, a bain-marie consists of a pan containing food placed inside a larger pan of warm (not boiling) water, surrounding the smaller pan with heat. Placed in an oven, a bain-marie generates steam for foods that require moist heat. Compare to double boiler.

BANYULS: A sweet fortified wine made in a place in southwestern France of the same name. Port would be an acceptable substitute if Banyuls is not available.

TO BARD: To wrap or cover meat or fish with strips of pork fat (fat back, salt pork etc.) to prevent it from drying out while cooking.

BÉCHAMEL SAUCE: A basic white sauce made by adding milk to a roux. The consistency of the sauce varies greatly depending on the proportions of butter, flour and milk used.

BEURRE MANIÉ: A paste consisting of softened butter and flour, usually in equal amounts, used to thicken sauces or soups. *Beurre manié* and roux are both thickening mixtures of butter and flour, but a roux is cooked beforehand and *beurre manié* is not.

TO BIND: Adding any of a number of substances, including flour, cornstarch, eggs, egg yolk, gelatin or cream, to a hot liquid in order to make it creamier.

TO BLANCH: Briefly immersing fruits, vegetables or variety meats (innards and extremeties) in boiling water and then in cold water to stop the cooking. This process makes it easier to remove peels and skins, rids food of impurities, and preserves the flavor and color of food before freezing.

BOUQUET GARNI: A combination of herbs either tied together or bound in cheesecloth and used to flavor soups, stews, etc. The bouquet garni is removed before serving. The classic combination of herbs is thyme, bay leaf and parsley, though myriad variations exist.

TO BRAISE: Cooking technique in which food (usually meat or vegetables) is browned, then cooked in a small amount of liquid in a covered pot over a longer period of time.

TO BROWN: To sauté a food in hot butter or oil over fairly high heat, giving a browned exterior while the interior remains tender.

CHOUX PASTRY: A simple but unique dough that is prepared on the stovetop by bringing water or milk to a boil, adding flour and then beating in several eggs to form a sticky paste. This is the classic puff pastry.

CLARIFIED BUTTER: Butter that has been melted slowly without stirring, then skimmed and decanted, leaving the milk solids and water in the pan. This liquid is pure butter fat and has a higher smoking point than whole butter, but less intense flavor.

TO CLARIFY: To remove any particles which interfere with the clear appearance of liquids (i.e. jelly or consommé), usually by straining or binding the impurities, often by adding and then straining out egg white.

CONSOMMÉ: A meat-based stock that has been reduced and clarified; it is used as the base for soups and sauces.

COULIS: A thick sauce consisting of puréed fruit, occasionally with lemon juice or sugar added.

COURT-BOUILLON: A flavorful broth made with clove-studded onion, celery, carrots, a bouquet garni, and occasionally lemon and garlic. Court-bouillon is most often used to boil different fish and meats.

CRÈME FRAÎCHE: A thickened cream with an incomparably smooth texture and nutty, not sour, taste. It is indispensable in French cuisine, particularly in sauces since it does not separate when boiled. If not readily available, crème fraîche can be simulated by adding 1tsp-1tbsp buttermilk to 1 cup heavy cream and letting the mixture stand at room temperature 8-24 hours until thickened. This will keep up to 10 days in the refrigerator.

CRÉPINE: French for pork caul, which is the inner membrane lining the animal's stomach. It is used to wrap around various sausages and meat dishes and does not need to be removed after cooking.

TO DEGLAZE: Using a liquid such as water, alcohol or stock to dissolve food particles in a pan after food has been roasted or sautéed in it. This liquid is used as the basis of the sauce which accompanies the food.

TO DEFAT OR DEGREASE: To skim or pour off the fat that results from cooking meat or soups, for example. This is often done before deglazing a cooking pan to make the sauce much lighter.

TO DICE: To cut fruit or vegetables into even, dice-like shapes. Traditional dice is between ¼ and ½ inch (.5 and 1 cm) in size.

DOUBLE BOILER: A double boiler consists of two pans that nestle into each other. The bottom pan is filled with simmering water and the top pan rests over, but not in, the hot water, providing gentle heat to melt or cook delicate foods like custards or sauces. Compare to bain-marie.

EMULSION: A combination of difficult-to-combine elements such as water and oil, achieved by adding the second ingredient a drop at a time while whipping continuously.

TO ENRICH A SAUCE: The finishing touch for many French sauces, this involves thickening and refining a sauce just before it is served by adding small pieces of very cold butter, or occasionally crème fraîche or egg yolk. This should be done off the heat, preferably by swirling the saucepan, but a whisk or wooden spoon may be used.

FATBACK: Fat from the back of a pig, used in its natural form, rather than salted or smoked. Compare to salt pork.

FILLET: Any boneless piece of meat or fish.

TO FILLET FISH: To separate the flesh of a fish from its bones to obtain fish fillets.

FINES HERBS: A mixture of finely chopped herbs, classically fresh parsley, chives, tarragon and chervil, usually added to dishes at the end of their preparation.

TO FLAMBÉ: To pour alcohol over food and light the alcohol, imparting a very special flavor. This can be a dramatic presentation or an earlier step in the cooking process.

TO GARNISH: Decorating a dish to make it more visually appealing with various edible elements; also refers to the accompaniment itself. Garnish varies from a single piece of parsley, to the additions to a soup, to entire dishes served with the main entrée.

TO JULIENNE: To slice foods, primarily vegetables, into thin, regular matchsticks; also refers to foods sliced in this way.

TO KNEAD: To thoroughly combine and work the components of a dough either by hand or with the dough hook of an electric mixer to produce a homogenous dough. It can take 15 minutes or longer to produce a smooth, elastic dough when kneading by hand.

LANGOUSTINE: Commonly, but inaccurately, called prawn, these crustaceans resemble tiny Maine lobster and are not to be confused with shrimp.

TO LINE: To cover the inside of a mold or pan with whatever ingredient is called for. For a charlotte, lady fingers would be used. For aspic, the mold would be lined with gelatin.

TO MARINATE: To soak meat, fish or other foods in a marinade (aromatic liquid) for a period of time to allow the meat or fish to develop a deeper, richer flavor and become more tender.

MELON BALLER: A special spoon shaped like a tiny bowl used to carve circles from melons and other fruits and vegetables.

MESCLUN SALAD: A mix of several varieties of young salad greens that may include radicchio, frisée, sorrel, arugula and others.

MIREPOIX: Diced combination of vegetables, usually including carrots, onions and celery, which are browned in butter and used to add flavor to stews, sauces, etc.

TO NAP: To cover food with a thin layer of its accompanying sauce.

PÂTÉ: A mixture of ground meats, pork fat, seasonings and sometimes vegetables ranging from smooth to coarse.

PINEAU: A sweet, white fortified wine made in the Cognac region of France. If this is unavailable, a mixture of grape juice and cognac may be substituted.

TO POACH: A method of cooking food by immersing it in hot, but not boiling, water or other liquid.

TO RECONSTITUTE: To add liquid to dried or dehydrated foods, such as powdered milk or dried fruits and vegetables.

TO REDUCE: The fundamental step in sauce preparation is to cook a mixture until much of the liquid has evaporated, resulting in a thicker and more intensely-flavored sauce.

TO REFRESH: A means of preventing foods from continuing to cook in their own heat either by immersing the cooking pan in cold water or running cold water directly onto the food.

TO ROAST: A slow method of cooking food uncovered in the oven, which allows tender meat or fish to brown and caramelize on the outside and remain moist on the inside.

ROUX: A combination of flour and butter used to thicken sauces. Unlike beurre manié, roux is cooked for several minutes before any liquid is added, and has different levels of readiness: light, medium and dark.

SALT PORK: Fat from the belly and sides of a pig that is cured with salt. It is often blanched to reduce its saltiness. Compare to fat back.

TO SAUTÉ: A method of cooking in a very small amount of hot oil or other fat, usually in an uncovered pan. Food may be lightly sautéed (see to brown), or cooked all the way through.

TO SCALLOP: To thinly slice meat, fish or crustaceans.

TO SEAR OR SEAL: To brown food very quickly, usually by sautéing it in pre-heated fat, so that its surface seals or locks in the food's natural juices.

TO SKIM: To remove any impurities (fat, foam) which form on the surface of a liquid.

TO STRAIN: To pour or press ingredients through a sieve or alternatively through a piece of cheesecloth in order to remove impurities, lumps, or seeds.

TO STEW: To cook by simmering food just covered in liquid for a prolonged length of time. Stew also refers to the resulting dish, which is usually savory, but can also consist of fruit.

TO SWEAT: A method of cooking vegetables, especially onions, or other ingredients over low heat in butter or oil until they are transparent, without letting them brown.

TOURNEDO: A very lean and tender cut of beef tenderloin, just 1 inch (2.5 cm) thick.

TRUFFLE JUICE: The liquid won during the process of drying the celebrated truffles. An excellent and less costly means of adding the flavor of truffles, it is available from gourmet shops. Truffle oil, high quality oil in which truffles have been steeped, is another alternative.

TO TRUSS: To sew the legs of a chicken or other bird to its body in order to preserve its shape during cooking; also used more loosely to refer to securing any meat in a compact form.

VERJUICE OR FRENCH VERJUS: A fermented liquid made from unripe fruit, usually grapes, and used in cooking.

The Participating Chefs

Lionel Accolas
Chef de Cuisine

Nicolas Albano
Maître Cuisinier de France

Marc Bayon
Maître Cuisinier de France
Finaliste Meilleur Ouvrier de France

Marcel Benoit
Chef de Cuisine

Michel Bignon

Jean-Pierre Billoux

Luce Bodinaud

Jean-Claude Bon
Maître Cuisinier de France

Jean-Paul Borgeot

Dominique Bouchet

Hubert Boudey

Maurice Brazier
Chef de Cuisine
Maître Cuisinier de France

Claude Calas
Maître Artisan Cuisinier
Vice-Président des Maîtres-Artisans

Jacques Chibois
Chef de Cuisine

Alain Darc

Ginette Delaive
Commandeur des Cordons-Bleus
de France

Maurice Dupuy

Roland Durand
Maître Cuisinier de France
Meilleur Ouvrier de France

Odile Engel

Gilles Étéocle
Maître Cuisinier de France
Meilleur Ouvrier de France

Jean-François Ferrié

Denis Franc

Jean-Maurice Gaudry
Maître Cuisinier de France

Pierre-Jean et Jany Gleize
Maîtres Cuisiniers de France

Charles et Philippe Godard
Maîtres Cuisiniers de France

Lionel Goyard
Chef de Cuisine

Jean-Pierre Lallement
Maître Cuisinier de France

Jean Lenoir
Maître Cuisinier de France
Finaliste Meilleur Ouvrier de France

Jean Claude Linget

Bernard Mariller
Chef de Cuisine

Manuel Martinez
Chef de Cuisine
Maître Cuisinier de France
Meilleur Ouvrier de France

Paul-Louis et Michel Meissonnier
Maîtres Cuisiniers de France

Christian Métreau
Chef de Cuisine

Jacques Muller
Maître Cuisinier de France

Daniel Nachon
Chevalier de l'Ordre du Mérite

Jean-Luis Niqueux
Chef de Cuisine

Alain Nonnet
Chef de Cuisine
Maître Cuisinier de France
Finaliste Meilleur Ouvrier de France

Angelo Orilieri
Chevalier du Mérite Agricole

Claude Ribardière

Michel Robert
Chef de Cuisine

Armand Roth
Chef de Cuisine

Roger Roucou
Président des Maîtres
Cuisiniers de France

Jean et Alain Rougié

Gérard Royant
Maître Cuisinier de France

Georges-Victor Schmitt
Chevalier du Mérite Agricole

Pierre Sébilleau
Chef de Cuisine

Dominique Toulousy
Maître Cuisinier de France

Gilles Tournadre

Jean Truillot
Chef de Cuisine

Jean Vettard
Maître Cuisinier de France

Pascal Vilaseca
Chef de Cuisine

Huguette Zarka
Commandeur de la Confrérie
des Cordons-Bleus

Index of Recipes

	Page		Page
Ardennes Ham Surprises	112	Jumbo Shrimp in Morel Sauce	84
Artichoke and Scallop Blinis	104	Kidney and Sweetbread Stew	116
Artichokes with Red Gamay	214	Kidney with Cockscomb	184
Asparagus Gratin	172	Kidneys with Juniper	14
Bay Scallop-Filled Zucchini Blossoms	182	Lacaune Blood Sausage with Apples	56
Belgian Endive	08	Lamb Sweetbreads with Green Bean Mousse	24
Brussel Sprouts and Mussels	124	Langoustine and Artichoke Medley	44
Cabbage au Gratin	80	Langoustine and Pasta Soufflé	216
Calamari Fettucini	196	Langoustine Papillotes with Foie Gras	90
Calf's Liver with Onion Fondue	32	Light Spring Ragoût	46
Cannellini Beans	212	Liver in Raspberry Vinaigrette	118
Carp in Reuilly Pinot Sauce	148	Liver Roulades with Endive	220
Char Mousse with Vegetable Julienne	34	Lobster and Basil Flan	158
Chestnut-Stuffed Cabbage	126	Maroilles Flan	10
Chicken Liver Cakes	40	Minced Endive with Tomato and Bacon	82
Chicken Liver Canapés	138	Morel Feuilleté	52
Clams à la Marinière with Thyme	16	Muenster and Cumin Turnovers	166
Crab Pouches with Basil Sauce	178	Mushroom Cake with Black Sauce	58
Crab Ravioli with Blue Crab Sauce	156	Old-Fashioned Beuchelle Tourangelle	142
Creamed Carrots	164	Oysters and Cucumbers au Gratin	108
Duck Foie Gras with Grapes	66	Pig's Foot Crépinettes	192
Duck Foie Gras with Green Puy Lentils	20	Porcini and Potato Gâteau	190
Eel Pâté à la Sologne	70	Porcini and Potato Pancake	50
Eel Stew with Red Wine	208	Porcini Darioles	100
Eggplant au Gratin	144	Porcini Tart	188
Escargot Casserole à l'Entre-Deux-Mers	48	Porcini-Stuffed Cabbage	106
Fennel Pie Amoureuse	154	Potato and Mushroom Gratin	162
Fillets of Sole Glacé	202	Potato and Prune Gratin	198
Foie Gras and Langoustine Brioche	136	Potato Petals with Porcini	62
Foie Gras with Asparagus Tips	176	Potato Puffs	132
Garenne Rabbit Pie	76	Potatoes au Gratin with Laguiole	88

	Page		Page
Pot-au-Feu with Snails and Cabbage	210	The Drunkard's Andouillette	78
Pumpkin and Rice Tian	102	Thrush Pie	54
Pumpkin au Gratin	98	Tongue and Sweetbread Navarin	36
Rice Milanese	200	Tongue Stew	218
Roasted Whole Veal Kidneys	28	Trout and Truffle Dumplings	204
Salmon and Mushroom Millefeuille	128	Truffle Pouches	96
Salmon Galette	122	Veal Kidneys with Fresh Mint	68
Sardine Pie	74	Veal Liver with Parsley and Asparagus	170
Sausage with Red Wine and Leeks	206	Veal Sweetbreads and Caramelized Onions	110
Sautéed Chanterelles with Flowering Zucchini	94	Veal Sweetbreads with Morels	174
Sautéed Foie Gras with Apples	86	Vegetables au Gratin	18
Sautéed Tripe à la Lyonnaise	42	Warm Oysters à la Landes	64
Sautéed Veal Sweetbreads	168	Zucchini and Clam Mousse	152
Sea Kale with Hollandaise Sauce	26	Zucchini Tourte	22
Seafood Ravioli	92		
Seared Foie Gras with Endive and Red Pepper	194		
Shallot Flan	150	**BASIC RECIPES**	
Shellfish with Lemon-Butter Sauce	140	Beurre Blanc (Beurre Nantes)	224
Single-Crust Leek Pie	12	Court-Bouillon	222
Skate Fins with Vegetables	160	Crêpe Batter	223
Snail and Garlic Ravioli	72	Duck or Pigeon Stock	229
Snail Turnovers with Garlic Sauce	146	Filleting Fish	225
Sorrel Monkfish Pâté	114	Filleting Sole	226
Stewed Chanterelles with Fresh Pasta	60	Fish Mousse	233
Stuffed Artichoke Hearts à la Rosmadec	186	Fish Stock	230
Stuffed Cabbage à la Belle Meunière	38	Langoustine Consommé	231
Stuffed Cabbage à la Charentais	30	Madeira Sauce	227
Stuffed Mushrooms	180	Pasta Dough	234
Stuffed Peppers with Tomato Coulis	134	Pork Stock	235
Sweetbreads à la Veronique	130	Puff Pastry	228
Sweetbreads with Asparagus	120	Short Pastry	232